CAN YOU MEOW THAT AGAIN?

Un animal De Compagnie

CAN YOU MEOW THAT AGAIN?

The Ultimate Cat Owners' Guide to Communication and Training

Copyright © 2022 by Un Animal De Compagnie

All rights reserved.

It is not legal to reproduce, duplicate, or transmit any part of this document in either electronic means or in printed format. Recording of this publication is strictly prohibited and any storage of this document is not allowed unless with written permission from the publisher except for the use of brief quotations in a book review.

ISBN: 9798838496584

This is for you, who believed in me.

For those of you wondering if it's you.

The answer is yes.

TABLE OF CONTENTS

Introduction	1
Enjoy Your Gift	5

Chapter 1
More Than Words: How Your Cat "Talk" to You — 7

    The Glossary of Mews: Cat Vocalizations Defined — 18

Chapter 2
Who's Your Kitty? A Guide to Cat Personalities — 23

    Cat Breeds and Personalities — 23
    Cat Personalities by Age — 30
    The Feline Five: Common Cat Personality Types — 32
    Cat Personality Quiz — 33
    Results: — 36
    FAQs about Cat Personalities — 37

Chapter 3
Human Training: How to Be the Best Cat Owner You Can Be — 39

    Becoming a Cat Owner: How Much Are You Willing to Compromise? — 39

The Cons and Pros of Having a Cat	41
Cat Owner Personality Quiz: What Kind of Cat Owner Are You?	42
Results:	44
When a Cat Adopts You: What Should You Do If You Find a Stray?	45
Consider Fostering First: Help Cats in Need While You Help Yourself	47

Chapter 4
Kitty Tricks: You CAN Train Your Cat! — 49

What Do You Really Want to Teach Your Cat?	50
What If My Cat Is Not Interested?	52
How to Train Your Cat to Walk on a Leash	54
Clicker Training: Cool Tricks Your Cat Can Learn	57
How to Bond with Your Cat	59

Chapter 5
Living the Cat Life: Cat Problems and How to Solve Them — 61

Why Playing with Your Cat Is Essential	62
Common Behavior Problems in Cats	64
Why Does My Cat…?	70

Chapter 6
Bathroom Blues: Solving Common Litter Box Issues — 81

Does Your Kitty Have Litter Issues?	81
Behavioral Problems and Litter Box Issues	82
What Type of Litter Box Should You Get?	83

    Cat Litter: The Good, the Bad, and the Ugly   86
    Why Pine Pellets Are Purr-fect for the Litter Box   88

Chapter 7
Welcome Home, Kitty: A Guide for Bringing Your New Pet Into Your Household   91

    Rescue vs. Shelter: What's the Difference?   91
    What Should You Know Before Getting a Cat?   93
    Setting Up a Safe Environment for Your Cat   94
    How to Feed Your Cat   96
    How to Find a Vet (and Make Your First Vet Visit)   98
    Preventative Healthcare for Your Cat   99
    Playtime Tips for Your Cat   103
    Your Cat's Needs: Different Approaches for Different Ages   104
    Tips for Multi-Cat Households   105

Chapter 8
Indoor vs. Outdoor: What's Perfect for Your Cat?   109

    Factors to Consider in Deciding Whether to Let Your Cat Outside   109
    The Pros and Cons of Keeping Your Cat Indoors vs. Letting Your Cat Outside   110
    How to Decrease Risks for Outdoor Cats   112
    Best of Both Worlds: Building a Cattery   113

Chapter 9
Pet Food Problems: Why You Should Consider a Raw Diet for Your Cat   115

Pet Health Problems and the Pet Food Industry	116
A Holistic Approach: The Raw Food (Carnivore) Diet	118

Chapter 10
Feline 911: A Survival Guide for Cat Owners — 121

Moving to a New Home	121
Vacation Care for Your Cat	123
Emergency Vet Services and Feline First Aid	124
Cat First Aid Tips	125
Final Words	129
Also By	133
Resources	135

INTRODUCTION

> "I believe cats to be spirits come to earth. A cat, I am sure, could walk on a cloud without coming through."
>
> – Jules Verne

If you're reading this book, we're going to take an educated guess and say you love cats.

That's wonderful! We love cats, too.

Many cat owners, aspiring cat owners, and cat lovers have come to an understanding: Cats will be cats. These beautiful, intelligent creatures are typically described as low-maintenance, independent, even aloof, with little to no need for their humans except where food is concerned. In fact, a number of non-cat owners claim that cats aren't capable of the levels of affection, recognition, and love that dogs are – and furthermore, they simply can't be trained.

However, most cat owners know nothing could be further from the truth. Cats are loyal, smart, and loving companions who enrich our lives in countless ways. Any cat lover will proudly defend the emotional intelligence of felines until they run out of breath.

But can you actually train a cat? The general consensus is that it's simply not possible.

Luckily, that's not true either. Because – believe it or not – all cats are trainable.

Now, when we talk about "training" cats, it's not exactly like dog training. It can be a bit more challenging, but you can teach your cat to respond to voice commands, walk on a leash, and even perform tricks. More importantly, you can learn to understand what your cat is trying to tell you so that humans and their adorable kitty overlords can live in harmony.

Who Is This Book For?

If you love cats, this book is for you.

Maybe you've always wanted a cat and you're finally in a position to get one, but you're worried about how to introduce a furry member of the family and whether you'll be able to care for your new cat the right way.

Maybe you're a veteran cat owner, you've just adopted a cat with behavioral issues you have never dealt with before, and you're not sure how to solve the problem.

Maybe you're a one-cat family and want to expand the number of felines in your household, but you're concerned that your spoiled princess or prince might not be as excited about a new kitty as you are.

Maybe your cat is pregnant and you've never cared for newborn kittens before.

Or maybe you just adore your feline companion(s) and want to improve human-cat relations.

Introduction

Regardless of your situation or the age and number of cats you have – if you love them, you'll gain a lot from this book.

Experienced cat owners will enjoy learning more about how cats communicate. And you may believe that you can't teach an old cat new tricks, but we'll talk about some cat-friendly tricks, gentle teaching methods through positive reinforcements, and cat-specific ideas to improve the bond between you and your feline. You may even be able to leash-train your kitty (yes, it can be done!).

Beginner/new cat owners will be able to create a strong foundation for a long and happy life with cats. You'll learn about the dos and don'ts of cat ownership, how to introduce new cats to a household, the most effective and non-stressful (for both you and your cat) methods for improving cat behavior, and more.

If you're a new cat owner or cat-owner-to-be, don't let the medical information in this book scare you. We'll explain how to spot signs of illness or injury in your cat, ensure that you have a trusted veterinarian and emergency care resources at hand, and the best preventative measures you can take against injury and illness.

A Note on Kitty Pronouns

The proper pronouns to use in reference to cats may be something of a controversial topic. Cats may be male or female, so referring to all cats as "he" or "she" feels like something is missing – especially when reading about *your* cat, who may be male or female. While they/them is gender-neutral, the use of this pronoun can get repetitive.

And we certainly would not refer to your cat (or any cat) as "it"!

For the purposes of this book, we will refer to cats alternately as he/him, she/her, or they/them. Whatever pronoun is used, you can rest assured that, yes, we are indeed talking about *your* cat.

Who Are the Authors?

Caring cat owners are discerning about whose advice they listen to when it comes to their beloved felines – as they should be. Of course, you can find countless resources from veterinarians, animal experts, celebrity trainers, and other trusted authorities on cat behavior and cat training.

So, why should you read this book?

We, the authors, are a group of pet experts from all walks of life and many levels of experience. We are pet behaviorists, pet coaches, pet trainers, and veteran pet owners. Some of us work or have worked in rescue centers or animal shelters. Some of us own pet stores.

But we all have this in common: We adore pets.

Collectively, we've seen a lot of poor pet owner behavior. Probably too much. After we met in a Facebook group and shared our experiences with misunderstood, mistreated, and even abused cats, we decided to create a series of books designed to help keep cats out of shelters and rescue centers – and get them into caring forever homes where they'll be understood and loved.

Our mission is to educate cat owners and help them build better relationships with their animal companions so that no cat gets left behind.

Now, let's dive right into the first chapter, where you'll learn how cats communicate and empower yourself to understand your pet right "meow"!

ENJOY YOUR Gift

In appreciation for your purchase, we are offering you a FREE copy of MEAL PREP 101 - The Secret to Raw Feeding for Busy Pet Owners.

Are you interested in feeding your pet a raw diet but aren't sure where to start? This book has got you covered!

Scan Me
To Claim a Free Book

Download this *FREE* guide to discover:

- ✧ The benefits of raw feeding.
- ✧ When to feed your pet raw food.
- ✧ The truth about pet food advertising.
- ✧ How to prepare easy recipes for your dog and cat.

CHAPTER 1

MORE THAN WORDS: HOW YOUR CAT "TALK" TO YOU

> "A cat can be trusted to purr when she is pleased, which is more than can be said for human beings."
>
> – William Ralph Inge

Just like humans, cats communicate in two primary ways: through vocalization and body language.

Unfortunately, we cat owners can't obtain an exact transcript of what our cats are saying. Google Translate has yet to introduce its cat-to-human setting, and as far as we know, cats aren't interested in taking a class for Human as a Second Language.

The good news is that cats can be understood. In the same way that you can learn to analyze people through a combination of verbal and non-verbal cues, you can interpret your cat's feelings, needs, and desires when you know what their vocalizations and body language mean.

The following is a comprehensive guide to all things cat, translated into human for your convenience.

Strike a Pose: What Your Cat's Body Language Says

They say a picture is worth a thousand words. This holds true when it comes to your cat, who will give you far more visual cues to what he or she is trying to communicate than sounds ever could. While cats lack the musculature that humans and dogs have to form a wide range of expressions (for example, cats cannot truly smile), their overall physical presentation can certainly indicate happiness, anxiety, fear, boredom, aggression, and much more.

Cat body language can be read in their eyes, ears, whiskers, tail, body shape, and physical actions. Here's what to look for in your cat when you want to gauge their mood without being able to ask them outright how they're doing.

Eyes – The Windows to Your Cat's Soul

Your cat's eyes are not just beautiful – they're also amazing. Cats can see in the dark, and their eyes are highly expressive, especially their pupils.

They can stare for a long time without blinking. And when you look into your cat's eyes, you can get strong hints about what they're thinking. Here are some common cat eye movements that can help you get a read on your kitty:

Slow Blink: This famous cat expression, adored by cat owners and internet meme writers everywhere, indicates trust, relaxation, and love. And while returning a cat's meow may not make any sense to your feline friend, returning the slow blink lets them know that you love them, too.

Woogy Eyes: Sometimes, a cat's eyes will fly open far wider than usual, and their pupils will suddenly dilate to nearly fill the iris-like someone has just flipped their crazy switch. This signifies stimulation, and it can mean a few different things depending on the context. It may be a sign of fear (in which case you should offer comfort and reassurance). It may indicate excitement (in which case you should continue playing because your cat likes it). Or, it may signal that your cat has spotted prey and is preparing to pounce on it (in which case you should hope that the prey is not you).

Snake Eyes: Have your cat's pupils suddenly narrowed to slits, with the eyes wide open and fixed on a single point? Snake eyes can mean that your cat feels aggressive or may become angry soon. In many cases, narrowed pupils occur in territorial circumstances when cats feel that another cat (or a human or other animal) is encroaching on their space. So back away and allow the cat to relax – or if two cats are involved, separate them as quickly as possible.

Ears - Antennae for Cat Radio

The ears are among the most expressive body parts cats have. A cat's ears can swivel in all directions, lie flat, perk up, and even move independently when expressing their mood. What's more, cats' ears twitch a lot! They can hear far more sounds than humans, up to 1.6 octaves above our range, and often when their ears twitch, it means they're angling them around to focus on a sound. Here are some of the ear movements your cat might make and what they could mean:

Point! Point! When a cat's ears point straight up to the sky, she's alert and catching signals. This usually indicates excitement or the detection of prey (sometimes both!).

Slouched & Chill: Forward-resting ears mean that your cat is calm and relaxed. She's confident in her surroundings and couldn't be happier—unless there's a treat in the near future.

Planking: Flattened ears signify that your kitty is distressed and may be anxious or angry.

Twitchy: The twitching of your cat's ears can mean many things. They might be excited to see you, checking out a potential toy, or attempting to hone in on that prey-like sound they just heard. More problematically, your cat's ears may twitch for health-related reasons. Pests like fleas, mites, or lice can make a cat's ears itchy, or they might twitch their ears due to discomfort from an ear infection or a growth. We'll discuss this potential symptom in more detail in a later chapter.

Whiskers – More than the Cutest Mustache

Whiskers are very important to your cat. They don't just look pretty... They also help your kitty get around in more ways than one. Whiskers allow your cat to feel textures, figure out distance, directions, sizes, and more. Your cat uses their whiskers to protect their eyes, judge how far away their food is, and figure out whether they can jump onto or into things. Here's what your cat's whiskers may be saying, depending on where they are:

Happy Rainbow: When your cat is in a relaxed, contented, or happy state, their whiskers are composed in a neutral arc with natural drooping slightly to the sides.

The Peacock: Excitement and interest pull a cat's whiskers forward and fan them out, like a peacock displaying his plumage. A bout of the zoomies might follow this display!

Retracting the Feelers: If your cat's whiskers pull back, watch out. This signifies anything from anxiety to aggression, depending on how flat the whiskers are against their face. A full retraction means that kitty is likely to lash out at any second.

Tail – The Divining Rod of Feline Moods

Of all the body language cats tend to use, the majority centers on their tails. A cat's tail is incredibly expressive, capable of various positions and movements that can mean many things. One thing you should note is that, while cats and dogs can make similar motions with their tails, they usually do not mean the same thing for a cat as they do for a dog! Look for these tail movements and positions to help you better understand what your cat is trying to tell you:

The Swoop: In this neutral tail position, for standing cats, the tail hangs down loosely and may curve up a bit at the end, depending on the breed. For seated or reclined cats, the neutral position is curled loosely around them.

Straight-Up: If your cat's tail points up high and her fur is smooth and relaxed, she's happy and affectionate. A quivering, high-pointing tail is a sign of excitement or anticipation.

Sad Dog Tuck: When a cat is anxious or afraid, she'll lower her tail. When she is highly nervous, she may curl her tail tightly and tuck it under her body to make herself as small a target as possible, similar to a frightened dog.

Super Quivering: If your cat holds her tail erect and she's quivering all over, with maybe a few excited twitches at the end, she's very excited. She may just be happy to see you, or she might start quivering her tail when you're about to fill her food dish or give her a treat.

Twitch and Flick: While this position resembles quivering, a high-pointing tail that twitches rapidly at the end means that your cat is not feeling particularly receptive and wants you (or whatever person/pet she's facing) to back off before she wrecks your stuff.

Bottle Brush: Long-tailed cats, even short hair breeds, have the impressive ability to poof their tails out to double their original size. If your kitty is suddenly sporting a fluffy tail, they feel threatened—and it's time for you to identify and remove the threat.

The Thumper: Dogs wag their tails when they're happy, but if your kitty's tail is wagging quickly back and forth or thumping on the floor, beware – she is not happy. Cats wag or thump their tails when they are upset, anxious, or feeling threatened by something.

Love Wrap: If your cat rubs against your legs and wraps their tail around you, this is a great sign – they are showing you some love and affection, letting you know that they're completely relaxed around you. Cats may also wrap their tails around another cat's tail for the same reason: they're saying, "you're my best friend, and I love you." A cat's tail wrap is just like a human hug!

The Slow Swing: When your cat's tail is swinging slowly from side to side, this means they're seriously concentrating on something. And that something is likely to be a toy or prey they're about to pounce on.

Sleepy Flick: When your cat is lounging, or in a light sleep, she may give a little flick of her tail, often in response to you coming into the room or calling her name. This is just an acknowledgment that she heard you and is aware of your presence – but she's not necessarily going to come if you call her. She's thinking about it, deciding if it's worth her while to get up from her comfy spot. She may need an enticement if you want her to move!

The Question Mark: This position is when your cat holds their tail up with an inward-facing curve at the end, forming a shape like a question mark... which, in essence, it is! The question mark tail means that your cat is happy and feeling friendly, but it also means they're inquisitive and curious about something. If they're investigating you, they may be wondering if you have something tasty on hand to offer them.

Curled Around: If your cat's tail is curled around their body while awake, they are not feeling good. Cats curl their tails around themselves as a defensive measure, so this position means they are anxious, uncomfortable, or possibly afraid.

The 45: Cats holding their tails at a 45-degree angle, straight out behind them and aligned with or slightly lower than their bodies, feel uncertain. If you approach a cat and they position their tail this way, they may be interested but guarded. Take it slow and offer a hand, then wait for the cat to come to you.

Low Curve: The lower your cat's tail, the more uneasy she feels. If your cat's tail is hanging down and curved up clearly at the end, like a ski slope, she's feeling a bit defensive or slightly afraid. She may welcome some comforting head scratches in this case.

Body Shape – Common Cat Yoga Positions

You can tell a lot about your cat by the way they choose to sit or lie down. Here are some common cat poses you might find your kitty striking, along with what they mean:

Ball of Cat: A kitty who's enjoying a nice, deep sleep will curl into a tight ball with their heads tucked in or tilted slightly upward, forming an almost perfect circle of happy fur.

Do Not Disturb: The Ball of Cat may loosen after a while, and kitty's paws will fold across her face. Aside from being completely adorable, this pose means, "don't you dare wake me up, human. I'm having a lovely dream about mice." A cat roused from the Do Not Disturb state will not be a happy cat.

Egyptian Statue: This seated pose, with their head erect and tail curled around their legs, often with closed eyes and a contented expression, means they are relaxed (and probably thinking about sleep).

Cat Loaf: Perfect for quick catnaps, this position has your kitty seated with his eyes closed in contentment and his front paws tucked in. He's still alert to his surroundings, but a little extra sleep never hurts!

Murder Sprawl: Look at that sweet, adorable kitty on her back, grinning with her paws splayed out to the sides. Don't you want to pet that furry belly? Watch out! She may be waiting for you to come in for a stroke so she can catch you in her trap. If your cat rolls onto their back and lies there looking at you adorably, we recommend a string toy in place of a belly pat unless you want your hand bunny-thumped into submission. However, some cats *do* enjoy a good belly rub, so feel free to test this at least once and see how your cat responds.

Flying Kitty: This deep sleep position transforms your cat into Superman, with both front and back paws stretched out fully while lying flat on their belly. The Flying Kitty is ultra-relaxed, content, and has no fear or anxiety that danger is lurking nearby.

Water Bottle: There's nothing like the feeling of a warm cat snuggled on top of you, trusting and asleep. Cats are aware that limbs often move around, so if they climb into bed with you, they'll choose to sleep on your flattest, most available surface, usually your chest or back. This means your kitty trusts and loves you enough to fall asleep, knowing that you'll protect them.

Physical Actions – From Biscuits to Bumping

A kitty in motion may be up to anything! If you're wondering why your cat does the things they do, here are some of the answers to the meaning behind common cat actions:

Making Biscuits: Kneading is an instinctive behavior in cats, starting almost from birth. Nursing kittens use this pressing, open-and-close motion with both paws against their mothers to stimulate milk flow. It's a comforting action, and juvenile or adult cats will knead anything soft that's close to their humans (or the humans themselves) as a way to relax before going to sleep.

Rub-a-Dub-Dub: Rubbing and cats go hand in hand – many cats seem to be constantly rubbing against something, whether it's a piece of furniture, the closest set of legs, or your face while you're holding them (which, by the way, is irresistibly precious). While this action is a sign of affection, it's really more than that. The scent glands located on a cat's cheeks leave their scent behind as they rub – so if your kitty nuzzles your face, she's marking you as her territory.

The Headbutt: Some cats will bump their heads into you like a furry, not-very-aggressive battering ram. This head-bumping is similar to rubbing, as there are more scent glands on a cat's head. It can signify a bonding attempt. However, a friendly headbutt from your kitty might also mean that he's demanding skritches, so be sure to oblige.

And Beyond...

The most powerful way to understand your cat is by combining these non-vocalized cues so that you can interpret your cat's overall state of mind. Below, we'll explore the various body language tells that will inform you whether your cat is happy, about to murder something, or somewhere in between.

Your Cat Is Happy/Relaxed When...

- ✧ Pupils are at normal size, eyes are relaxed or half-closed
- ✧ Ears and whiskers are natural and at rest and may droop slightly forward
- ✧ Tail is loose and hanging down, with flattened fur and little to no movement
- ✧ Seated upright with head up and back straight, or lying down with belly showing

Your Cat Is Playful When...

- Eyes are wide and pupils are enlarged/dilated, usually fixed on a single point
- Ears point up and forward with an alert appearance
- Tail held either down or straight up, but with a twitching end
- Seated with head in motion and gaze alert, or crouched down at the front with the hind end raised in the air (this is a classic pre-pounce stance!)

Your Cat Is Nervous/Frightened When...

- Eyes look "playful" (wide with dilated pupils) but change their focus as the cat looks around
- Ears may either flick rapidly as they listen for potential warning sounds or draw down until they're pointing to the sides or lying flat against the head
- Tail is stiff and pointing straight up (may be bottle brushed) or curled around the body in a protective stance
- Crouched, tucked-in position or standing on all fours with their back arched and fur fluffed out

The Glossary of Mews: Cat Vocalizations Defined

If you're like most cat lovers, when your cat meows at you, your response is either to ask what's wrong (as if the cat will suddenly answer in perfect English) or meow right back (as if mimicking the sound will help you puzzle it out). Predictably, neither of these methods results in actual human-to-cat conversation – although it does make us happy.

Cats first begin to meow as kittens to get their mothers' attention. As they grow, they stop using this type of vocalization to communicate with other cats. However, they still meow at humans because they've learned that this sound gets attention. They've also figured out that humans aren't especially observant. So, when your cat meows at you, they want to draw your attention to something that's obviously escaped your notice.

What, exactly, are they saying? The good news is that you don't have to guess when you know how to analyze a meow. Here's your complete list of cat vocalizations and their appropriate meanings to help you really "get" your cat.

Scan Me
To Listen Now

The Meow-Meow: This "normal" meow is more versatile for a cat than "Aloha" is for a native Hawaiian. For a cat, the regular, everyday meow may be a greeting for their favorite human or an announcement that they'd like to call attention to the lack of cat treats in the vicinity. A simple "meow" might be an objection – it's too hot, it's too cold, the other cat has stolen my favorite sleeping spot. It could be a command – for example, to remove said other cat from the aforementioned favorite sleeping spot.

It's also interesting to note that the normal meow is rarely, if ever, directed at other cats. In domesticated cats, this type of vocal communication is reserved solely for humans.

Keep in mind that just as no two cats are alike, and no two "normal" meows are alike. Your cat's normal vocalization may sound like another cat's triumphant yawp after she's finally caught that mouse that's been evading her for weeks. It typically doesn't take long to determine what your cat usually sounds like, as opposed to when he's trying to tell you something.

The Little Mew: Common in younger cats, this short and plaintive sound means that kitty is lonely, bored, hungry, or all of the above.

The Soft Meow: A cat meowing with her mouth closed is a happy sound and is often meant as a greeting or statement of pleasure, such as "I am greatly enjoying my relaxation on this warm machine that you were just typing on a minute ago." The soft murp may end in a chirp if the cat is especially happy.

The Wow-Meow: An inquisitive vocalization, the wow-meow can sound very similar to the word "wow" when some cats make it. This meow starts at a low pitch and gets higher: *woo—OWW?* and usually means that your cat is curious about something (such as why the food bowl is empty or where the plastic bag he was chewing on a minute ago went).

The Machine Gun: This rapid-fire, almost frantic series of short mews is more common in younger cats and is a demand for immediate attention.

The Long, Sad Trumpet: An extended yowl that typically pitches up toward the end; this mournful sound is throatier than your cat's normal meow and usually indicates annoyance or objection. In short, kitty is displeased.

The Plaintive Yowl: Similar to the Long, Sad Trumpet but often louder and more insistent, this sound, followed by rapid glugging, means that your cat is about to yark up a furball.

The Yummy-Yummy-Yummy: Kittens and younger cats are the most likely to make this sound while eating, usually canned food. This vocalization sounds like your cat is saying "yummy, yummy, yummy" as she enjoys her food… but it's actually a warning that if anyone tries to take the enjoyable food away, there will be claws and teeth involved.

The Rumbling Engine: There are few things in life more satisfying than a purring cat. In general, purring indicates that your kitty is content; she's warm, happy, and feels safe and protected right where she is. Hence the reason many cat owners find themselves seated in the same awkward position until their legs cramp because they don't want to disturb the purring cat sitting on them. Some cats may even purr while they're eating or sleeping.

However, there are times when purring can indicate a problem. If your cat shows signs of discomfort, illness, or injury and begins to purr, this may be a self-comforting action to ease distress. You should consult your veterinarian if your cat is purring, and you've also identified signs of illness such as lack of appetite, hiding, or fever, as it might signify a health issue you can't detect.

The Bird-Cat: Chirps and trills are among the most adorable, heart-melting sounds that a cat can make, perhaps second only to the sweet mew of a tiny kitten. In fact, these sounds are directly associated with kittens – this is the vocalization a mother cat uses when she wants her kittens to follow her. And since cats seem to view humans as very large, exceptionally clueless kittens, she may aim this sound at you in hopes that you'll follow – usually to her tragically empty food bowl.

The Chattering Catty: A sound typically made by a cat sitting at a window, rapid chattering (which can sound like clicking or stuttering) is a prey response that means your kitty has spotted something alive and tasty outside. The sound is part mimicking kitty's prey and part frustration that he can't actually hunt the delicious treat that's just out of reach behind the glass or screen.

The Grumble-Growl: The growl of a cat can range from adorable to worrisome, depending on the size, temperament, and proximity of the cat to whatever she's angry at. If this sound isn't stopped by the appeasement of your cat's irritation, she'll often progress to the next vocalization on the list.

The Sizzling Steak: Cats hiss as a warning, usually after they've started with a growl. This display of fear, anger, or extreme annoyance may also include spitting and snarling.

The Unholy Caterwaul: Almost exclusively reserved for female cats, this distinctive, loud, and drawn-out cry is the sound of an unspayed female looking for a mate. On rare occasions, older cats might emit a caterwaul if they're disoriented or experiencing cognitive loss. So, if your kitty makes this noise and is not an intact female of prime reproductive age, you should consult your vet.

The Primeval Scream: Just as distinctive as the caterwaul, this piercing, rising shriek is usually the music of two cats fighting. Females may also scream like this during mating.

While learning to understand your cat, remember that every feline is different. While some nonverbal cues and vocalizations remain almost universal among cats, each cat will have a form of communication unique to them. The more time you spend with your cat, the better you'll be able to identify what they're trying to tell you – and the more fun you'll both have as your bond continues to grow.

In the next chapter, we present a guide to cat personalities, including our cat personality quiz! Read on to find out more about the many personalities of cats and which famous feline your kitty most resembles.

CHAPTER 2

WHO'S YOUR KITTY? A GUIDE TO CAT PERSONALITIES

> "Unlike the dog, the cat's personality is never bet on a human's. He demands acceptance on his own terms."
>
> – Lloyd Alexander

Anyone who utters "it's just a cat" has never met an actual cat. Every one of our feline friends has a distinctive personality that's all his or her own – and when you start spending just a little bit of time with cats, those personalities will come out and shine.

In this chapter, we'll talk about cat personalities and the many factors that shape them. We'll even include a cat personality quiz, so you can find out which well-known cat is closest to your kitty's unique personality.

Cat Breeds and Personalities

One influential factor in cat personality is their breed. Depending on which source you use, there are anywhere from thirty cat breeds (according to Encyclopedia Britannica) to seventy-three (according to The International Cat Association). What's more, many cats are mixed breed and may possess personality traits belonging to any number of cats in their ancestral lines.

While we can't cover all seventy-one recognized cat breeds, here's a look at the ten most common and most popular cat breeds and their associated personality types.

Domestic Shorthair

Hands-down the most common cat breed, with both American and British versions, the domestic shorthair is an "average cat" (although there is nothing average about any cat). They come in a massive array of sizes, colors, patterns, and statures, with the only physical things in common being their short, sleek coats and rounded paws and heads. They're generally mixed breed and might be black, white, or gray; tabby, tuxedo, calico, or tortoiseshell. Most domestic shorthairs are fantastic mousers as well.

The personalities of domestic shorthairs are just as varied as their colors and markings. In general, they're a playful and friendly breed with plenty of energy, especially at night when their hunting instincts kick in (beware of the 3 a.m. zoomies!). Whether they are quiet or vocal, calm or manic, domestic shorthairs are usually very social and make a good fit for any household.

Maine Coon

An unusually large cat breed that appears even bigger than they are thanks to their fluffy coats, the Maine Coon has big feet, a big appetite, and a big heart. Maine Coon coloring ranges from white to black and everything in between, including red, cream, brown, blue, and even silver or golden. They can be a solid color or patterned in tortoiseshell, calico, bicolor, tabby, shaded, or smoke.

These calm and friendly cats are exceptional hunters. Highly vocal and sociable, they love to "chat" and will often follow you around, led by their insatiable curiosity. Maine Coons have been known to teach themselves tricks to get their human's attention – so if you have one of these big, cuddly cats, they may be partially trained already!

Siamese

The distinctive appearance of the Siamese breed is a match to the unique personality traits of this cat type. Siamese cats are very smart, talkative, and just as sneaky and mischievous as the stereotypes imply – although they're far more affectionate than portrayed.

Siamese cats need lots of affection, stimulation, and social interaction with plenty of playtime. Although a Siamese can be trained, it comes down to whether or not they *want* to be trained. This breed has their own agenda, and it won't always align with yours.

Ragdoll

The large, beautiful, blue-eyed ragdoll cat is among the most devoted of breeds. Ragdolls have silky, fluffy fur and typically sport markings similar to the Siamese breed, including ear points and mittens. Their colors include cream, blue cream, frost, chocolate, red, seal, and lilac.

As implied by their names, ragdolls love to be held (although they don't actually flop like a ragdoll in your arms). They have a wide range of vocalizations, though many ragdoll cats aren't especially talkative, and they absolutely love to play. Ragdolls are easygoing and can get along just about anywhere.

Persian

One of the most recognizable cat breeds, the Persian is known by its squashed face and long, silky fur (which needs regular grooming!). Persian colors range from white and cream to brown and black with all colors in between, and their patterns can be seal point, smoke, shaded, tabby, calico, bicolor, or solid.

On the whole, Persians are a placid breed who love to lounge around, looking majestic. However, they are prone to sudden bursts of energy, even from what looks like a deep sleep, complete with running and rolling and stalking invisible enemies. Persians are a friendly and happy breed with a chilled-out personality, despite the occasional case of the zoomies, and love sleeping in bed with you.

Bengal

Perhaps the closest we can get to having a wild cat in the house, Bengals look like small leopards with their cream coats overlaid in dark spots and rosettes. This large-breed cat has a long body, smooth coat, thick neck, and big feet.

Bengals are one of the few breeds who truly enjoy the great outdoors. These highly intelligent, skilled hunters require a lot of exercise and playtime, but they reward you with their talkative, friendly nature and tons of affection. They can learn tricks easily and have exceptional memories. They're also one of the only cat breeds who are happy to go for a swim!

Sphynx

Another breed that is immediately recognizable by appearance, the hairless Sphynx may look broody and mysterious, but this cat is a

real snuggler (and not just because they lack fur). The Sphynx breed is always hungry and always willing to curl up in your nice, warm lap or alongside a furrier pet for warmth and companionship. They love to talk and make the most adorable squeaking sound when their naps are interrupted.

Sphynx cats are energetic and eager to perform. They're also perchers and will take any opportunity to jump on your shoulder. Since the Sphynx already loves doing tricks for your attention, they are often highly trainable.

Munchkin

"Cuteness overload" is one way to describe the Munchkin breed. These pint-sized balls of fluff with silky, plush fur are compact cats with long bodies and extra-short legs – and even when fully grown, the Munchkin still resembles a kitten.

The breed's personality is also kitten-like. Munchkins are energetic, fast-moving little guys and gals with a side-to-side running pattern that resembles a ferret. They love to jump, play, and cuddle, and their high intelligence means they need a lot of attention and mental stimulation.

One characteristic that's unique to the Munchkin breed is that they are hoarders – and like crows, they're particularly attracted to shiny objects. If you have a Munchkin in the house, keep an eye on your jewelry and baubles. If they start disappearing, it's time to look for your kitty's stash.

Scottish Fold

If we could describe the Scottish Fold in one word, it would be "round." This medium shorthair cat comes in all colors and patterns and is round all over – from the head with folded ears that blend right in to the big eyes, round legs, and short tail.

Just as their appearance suggests, Scottish Folds are a bundle of joy. Charming, sweet, easygoing, and affectionate, this breed gets along with everyone. You just have to ensure that you handle their tails gently because many Scottish Fold cats develop tail stiffness that can become painful when mishandled.

Abyssinian

The Abyssinian is a domestic shorthair breed with enlarged ears and a distinctive ticked tabby pattern. Ancient Egyptians revered this breed so much that they used to mummify them so their fallen humans could keep them in their tombs alongside them.

Abyssinian cats are highly intelligent and inquisitive, and they love to "help" you around the house. They are a talkative breed, frequently trilling their pleasure as they follow you just about everywhere. This breed loves playtime and, unlike most cats, can be taught to fetch. They desire your affection and shouldn't be left alone for long. Although Abyssinians are not

exactly lap cats, they show plenty of affection – and they also love other pets, as they're very sociable and friendly.

Russian Blue

Despite being named after a land known for its inhospitable climate, the Russian Blue is among the warmest and sweetest kitties you'll ever meet. Russian Blues have soft, extremely dense double coats of fur, making them appear larger than they are. They are solid color kitties, always dark gray with silver tips, and their characteristic brilliant green eyes make them gorgeous and friendly.

Russian Blues are loyal and love to follow you everywhere, often greeting you at the door when you come home. Highly sociable but shy with unfamiliar people, this kitty loves (and needs) lots of playtime. They are vocal breeds and are very persistent about having their needs met, so be prepared for a barrage of meows when their food bowl is empty!

Cat Personalities by Age

The age of your cat plays into their personality as well. Like humans, cats go through life stages that affect their mood, energy, and interests. Here's a look at the various life stages of cats and the personality traits you might expect to see with each one.

Kitten: The kitten stage lasts from birth to six months. Once kittens are old enough to move around independently, they are filled with boundless energy and endless curiosity. It's playtime all the time for a kitten (unless it's feeding time or nap time, of course!).

Juvenile (junior, teen): Juvenile cats, from six months to two years old, are still incredibly playful – but during this stage, they start to explore their boundaries. These teenage cats will often challenge any human or other pet for dominance, and as their hunting instincts kick in, they will stalk and pounce at everything.

Prime: While your cat is around 3 to 6 years old, they have a handle on the basics, and they've established their personalities. Cats in their prime are typically healthy and active, with a good balance of lounging, napping, and playing in random bursts at all times of the day (and night).

Mature: A middle-aged cat, from 7 to 10 years old, has settled in their ways and doesn't care for change. Mature cats can show heightened anxiety at times and will have lower levels of energy, but they still love to play when the mood strikes.

Senior: Older cats from 11 to 14 often develop a "grumpy old person" vibe and may be more irritated by annoyances than they used to be. At this stage, they're not as playful and might begin to develop health problems, such as hearing or vision loss and a decline in cognitive function. However, senior cats are typically affectionate and love to cuddle with their humans.

Geriatric: This stage of life at 15 years and up is when your cat will require a lot of care and attention, as well as regular checkups from the vet. Health and behavioral changes are common as your older cat seeks comfort, routine, and familiarity. Geriatric cats should always have immediate, easy access to food and water, with a litter box close by.

The Feline Five: Common Cat Personality Types

While cat owners and cat lovers around the world have known since the first cat decided that sticking around humans was mutually beneficial that cats have distinctive personalities, this phenomenon has never been officially recognized by science – until relatively recently, that is.

A study published in 2017 offers evidence that a cat is never "just a cat." "The 'Feline Five'" study identifies five distinct personality types that domestic cats exhibit. They are:

- **Agreeableness:** This describes cats who are, obviously, agreeable – those who are gentle, affectionate, and friendly with humans (as well as other pets... for the most part). Easy to please, they want nothing but yummies, lots of snuggles, and a warm place to sleep.

- **Dominance:** The "tomcat" personality type, a dominant cat wants nothing to do with other felines and will fight for their territory (and their humans).

- **Extroversion:** These curious kitties are highly active, ever vigilant, and will introduce themselves to new people, animals, and situations without hesitation.

- **Impulsiveness:** Impulsive cats have little regard for safety and may seem to live for the thrill, performing questionable actions just for the fun of it. These reckless felines are often in high spirits, whether they're shredding all the toilet paper or sleeping directly in the way of everything.

- **Neuroticism:** These feline versions of the Fear character from *Inside Out* worry about everything, from whether more food will ever reappear in their bowls to what that suspicious pile of dust is doing in the corner.

The Feline Five does not state that all cats can be slotted into one of these five categories. Rather, most cats possess a blend of personality traits from all five categories, with one or two classifications usually more dominant than the rest.

Cat Personality Quiz

What kind of personality does your cat have? Take this quiz and find out which of the Feline Five traits are most dominant in your cat – and which famous feline they are most like.

1. *What does your cat love to spend time doing?*

    a.   Eating and worrying about whether there will be more food in the immediate future

    b.   Checking out absolutely everything to make sure it's okay – new people, new sounds, new boxes, you name it

    c.   Playfully ruining cardboard, toilet paper, and the dinner you're trying to make

    d.   Attacking and/or hunting everything that moves

    e.   Lying around looking gorgeous and getting all the love

2. *What is your cat's reaction to string toys?*

    a.   What's this thing? Is it dangerous? Can I eat it?

    b.   Okay, I'll play with it, but are you sure you know how to use this, human?

    c.   Ooh, a dangly! I will bat it around until I get all tangled up in the… Wait, how do I get out of this?

    d.   KILL! KILL! KILL!

    e.   Aren't I adorable playing with this toy? I love this toy and I love you.

3. How is your cat most likely to react when you come home after being gone?

    a.   Runs up and demands you pay attention to the empty food bowl (unless they're asleep)

    b.   Comes to check you out for a minute, then goes back to whatever they were doing before

    c.   Can't wait to show you what a mess they've made while you were gone

    d.   Presents you with their latest kill while making sure you don't smell like another animal

    e.   Decrees that it's cuddle time now

4. There's an empty paper bag on the floor. Your cat...

    a.   Pokes at it, then looks at you as if to ask how this mysterious intruder got here

    b.   Immediately walks into the bag to check it out, then emerges to give the all-clear

    c.   Dives in headfirst and may spend several minutes rolling around and making a lot of crinkly noises before falling asleep

    d.   Ignores it because it's not moving and doesn't seem to be alive or a threat

    e.   Might slip in gracefully for a quick nap, but only once or twice because your lap or your bed is a much nicer place to sleep

5. How does your cat react when someone new comes to your place for the first time?

    a.   Eek! Run and hide! Unless the new human has treats...

    b.   Walks right up to the new arrival to sniff them and make sure they're okay

c. Goes into show-off mode, posing and pouncing as they make sure the new person is watching them. May chew on some of their stuff for a while, just for the heck of it

d. Doesn't especially acknowledge their presence – unless they're taking all your attention, in which case it's war

e. Loves their new friend, you, and everyone

6. Where does your cat love to sleep?

a. In their bed and nowhere else

b. Somewhere high up, where they can keep an eye on things

c. Usually any place that looks impossible to get comfortable, where they might fall off at any second

d. Anywhere they want to, and you can't stop them

e. Wherever you are, that's where they'll sleep too

7. It's storming outside. Your cat is...

a. Cowering somewhere, either as close to you as they can get or in a place so hidden you can't find them

b. Sitting at a window and staring watchfully outside, as if daring the storm to come any closer

c. Ignoring the whole thing because there are so many things they haven't played with yet

d. Stalking weak points of the house in case the weather drives some small, defenseless creature inside – straight to their waiting claws

e. Cuddling with you, as usual, because humans need comfort from scary storms too

Results:

Mostly **A**s

Garfield (neuroticism): Your cat loves comfort and food and worries when things get moved around or changed unexpectedly but is affectionate when pleased.

Mostly **B**s

Luna (extroversion): Wise and spirited as Sailor Moon's feline advisor, her namesake, your cat knows that you aren't that smart but will help you out by watching over you constantly.

Mostly **C**s

Danny (impulsiveness): Having much in common with the goofy "song-and-dance" cat from *Cats Don't Dance*, your cat will try anything once (or twice, or three times) and is just happy to be here, living their best life.

Mostly **D**s

Lucifer (dominance): The stepmother's evil cat from *Cinderella*, your cat wants everyone to know who's in charge (and it's him) but will defer to you in all things. Most of the time.

Mostly **E**s

Duchess (agreeableness): Like the aptly named lady cat in Disney's *The Aristocats*, your cat is gorgeous, spoiled rotten, and knows it. Gentle and loving, your cat exists for affection at all times and will give as much love as she receives.

FAQs about Cat Personalities

Why are cat personalities so different?

Far from having a hive mind, cats are unique in personality due to "a complex interaction between each cat's genetics and their experiences during development and in adulthood," according to Dr. Lauren Finka, author of the Feline Five study. In other words, cats' personalities – much like humans – are a combination of nature and nurture.

Are all cats lazy?

"Cats" and "lazy" are often synonymous because they sleep so much – usually averaging around 16 to 18 hours per day. However, cats don't sleep so much because they're bored and/or can't be bothered to do anything else.

You can see this sleeping pattern reflected in wild cats of all sizes. Although we keep cats as domestic pets, they still retain their instincts even when they're no longer necessary for survival... specifically, the instinct to hunt.

Cats expend massive amounts of energy while hunting. For wild cats, it's a matter of survival, but domestic cats "hunt" toys, sleeping spots, random bags or boxes, and sometimes even prey (if they can get to it). Following a "hunt," a cat's instinct is to sleep to conserve energy for the next hunt.

So, what we might view as lazy, cats view as strategic, smart, and perfectly normal.

Does my cat love me?

Because of their aloof, independent reputations, some believe that cats aren't capable of love. However, this simply is not true. Cats share many of the same emotions as humans, including the desire to be around their people and the enjoyment of their humans' presence. While it's true that being fed and sheltered is important for cats, they also truly love to be with us.

Some signs that your cat loves you include:

- ✧ The slow blink, a widely known sign of affection for cats
- ✧ Following you around the house
- ✧ Treating you like you're "just one of the cats" through rubbing, grooming, and sleeping near you – an indication that they feel safe around you
- ✧ Kneading, purring, and other obvious affectionate behaviors (such as curling up in your lap for a snooze

Are cats fully domesticated?

Dogs have lived with people for far longer, historically speaking, than cats have. According to scientists, the domestication of dogs is estimated to have occurred between 18,000 to 30,000 years ago (Stony Brook University, 2017), while the first sign of domestication for cats lies in Egyptian paintings, statues, and tombs that date back only around 4,000 years (Driscoll, 2007).

For this reason, many scientists believe that cats aren't fully domesticated. It would explain why a cat's wild instincts are still present in house cats, even when they no longer need to hunt for food or protect themselves from predators.

Now that you know more about cat personalities and the unique traits of your feline companion, you can approach training your cat with his or her personality in mind.

In the next chapter, we'll talk about the many ways people go about obtaining cats and what type of cat you're best suited for, including our Cat Owner Personality Quiz. Keep reading!

CHAPTER 3

HUMAN TRAINING: HOW TO BE THE BEST CAT OWNER YOU CAN BE

"As every cat owner knows, nobody owns a cat."

– Ellen Perry Berkely

Whether you're a current cat owner, you haven't had a cat in a while for whatever reason, or you're thinking about getting your first cat, it never hurts to know more about having cats as part of your household. The more you know about yourself as a cat owner, the easier it will be to create a harmonious cat-human environment where neither you nor your cat(s) is stressed by the relationship.

Becoming a Cat Owner: How Much Are You Willing to Compromise?

You may already know the answer to this question if you're a veteran cat person (and quite likely, your answer may be along the lines of "I'll do anything for my cat"). But if you're just entering the wonderful world of cat parenting, you need to take a realistic look at your comfort levels and tolerance for typical cat behavior. Make sure you're ready for the responsibility – and the rewards – that come with inviting a cat into your life.

Too often, rescues and shelters are populated with cats given up by their owners through no fault of their own. Some of these common complaints include that the cat:

- Meows too much
- Rubs against people's legs
- Doesn't like being picked up or petted
- Isn't "cuddly" enough
- Gets scared frequently and spends most of their time hiding
- Makes too much noise at night
- Doesn't like a new partner/person in the house

Cat "nuisance" behaviors always have an underlying cause, and they're usually because the cat either doesn't feel well physically or is unhappy, nervous, or scared. If you are going to have a cat, you must have patience and the willingness to work through any behavioral issues that your new cat may have – and you must be prepared to keep your cat even if someone new in your life doesn't like them or is allergic to cats.

So, potential new cat owners: Please don't get a cat unless you're willing to take full responsibility for these complex, loving animals… and to do everything you can to make them truly a part of your home.

The Cons and Pros of Having a Cat

As with everything in life, there are advantages and disadvantages to bringing a cat into your life. We're going to list the downsides first because there are so many more benefits that outweigh them for those who are ready to embrace cat life.

Cons

- Cats are an additional household expense since you'll need to provide food, cat litter, toys, and a few larger items in the beginning (litter box, cat bed, etc.)
- Veterinarian bills can be expensive
- Litter boxes don't exactly smell like roses
- Some cats may have behavioral issues you'll need to address
- If you're looking for an outdoorsy pet to take camping and hiking, a cat may not be the best choice

Pros

- Cats are largely independent and low-maintenance compared to other pets
- Cats are equally happy in big spaces or small ones, like apartments
- You'll never have to worry about mice with a cat in the house
- Cats are highly entertaining (especially when they get the zoomies!)
- Posting pictures of your cat to social media makes everybody happy

- There is scientific proof that cats lower stress levels and blood pressure and might even reduce the risk of heart attacks and stroke (Qureshi, 2009)
- Cats provide nurturing, companionship, and unconditional love

Cat Owner Personality Quiz: What Kind of Cat Owner Are You?

Finding the right cat for you and your household goes a long way toward enjoying a long and happy relationship with your new feline friend. So, what kind of cat owner are you, and which type of cat will fit into your home like a glove? Take our quiz and find out!

1. What are you most looking forward to doing with your cat?

a. Having a nice cuddle when you get home from work, maybe watching some TV together

b. Anything outdoors (cats like going outside, right?) or anything that involves lots of fun and activity. Can I take my cat on hikes?

c. I want to spend hours and hours snuggling, brushing, spoiling, and taking pictures of my darling kitty!

d. Hopefully, my new cat will love all my other animals. I'd love to have a cat who'll make friends with my dog/iguana/parakeet/ferrets or other cats.

e. I just hope we can find a cat who will love the kids and be patient with them.

2. You love cats that are:

   a. Not too big, not too small
   b. Definitely on the big side
   c. Beautiful and unique
   d. Any shape, size, or texture
   e. Family-sized

3. Your cat's ideal personality is:

   a. Aloof and independent (but still loves you)
   b. Up for anything, anytime, and anywhere
   c. Prince or princess of all they survey
   d. Please be my friend, whatever you are!
   e. The most chill, sweetest kitty ever

4. Who is around to interact with your cat?

   a. Me and/or a partner, or often no one is home
   b. Someone in the family is usually around
   c. Me. Possibly other people, but I'm going to spend so much time with my cat.
   d. If we're not home, there are plenty of other pets to keep kitty company
   e. Family of all ages

5. When a stranger comes to your house, you'd like your cat to:

   a. Wander off. They're not interested in strangers
   b. Be busy playing, though they don't mind meeting someone new
   c. Just be their beautiful, spoiled selves, like always

d. Check out the new person, especially if another animal friend comes with them

e. Love the new human, even if they're small and a bit grabby

6. What would be the best thing for you about having a cat?

a. Knowing they're always there for me after a long day

b. All the memories we'll make out there in the world

c. Absolutely everything, but especially snuggles and sleeping together

d. When they fall in love with my other pets

e. Having a loving, affectionate friend for my children

Results:

Mostly **A**s

The Welcomer: You're best suited to enjoy a cat who can take care of themselves, thank you very much, and don't mind if you have to leave for a while – but still gets warm and snuggly when you walk through the door. The best cat breeds to welcome into sharing your home are the **Domestic Shorthair, Russian Blue, Persian, Maine Coon, or Scottish Fold**.

Mostly **B**s

The Adventurer: Your ideal kitty companion is big, bold, and comes with loads of personality. They love long walks and might even join you on your next hike. Your home has plenty of room for your new best friend, too! The best cat breeds to join you in your adventures are the **Bengal, Abyssinian, or Maine Coon**.

Mostly **C**s

The Spoiler: You're looking for that special "only cat" to shower with love and attention, who loves being picked up, petted, brushed, and otherwise fussed over. In return, you'll devote yourself to your beloved feline. The best cat breeds for you to bring home and spoil rotten are the **Siamese, Sphynx, Munchkin, Ragdoll, or Persian.**

Mostly **D**s

The Zookeeper: Animals are everything to you, so in addition to your kitties (oh, you'll have more than one), you might have any number of pet companions around… and you'd like them all to get along! The best cat breeds for your all-species-welcome household are the **Ragdoll, Abyssinian, Russian Blue, Domestic Shorthair, Scottish Fold, or Sphynx.**

Mostly **E**s

The Nurturer: It's most important for you to have a true family cat who loves attention and will snuggle the baby or doesn't mind the occasional accidental tail-pull from a toddler. The best cat breeds to bring into your family are the **Domestic Shorthair, Ragdoll, Munchkin, Russian Blue, or Siamese.**

When a Cat Adopts You: What Should You Do If You Find a Stray?

A surprising number of people become cat owners when a stray cat "adopts" them. This happens most often with cats who previously belonged to a home that, for whatever reason, they can no longer return to. However, some feral cats may also seek human interaction, even if they've never lived in a house before.

A stray or feral cat who's hanging around your house may be taking shelter either nearby or on the premises, such as under your porch or in your garage. Friendlier strays who are more recently used to people might even come onto your porch or walk right up to your door.

So, what should you do if a stray cat adopts you and you're willing to take them in?

Leave out food: Generally speaking, a stray cat is a hungry cat. If you'd like them to hang around, leaving food out for them will usually keep them coming back. Like any animal (including those of the human variety), cats will always choose a ready food source over scrounging or hunting.

Make sure the cat is actually a stray: Before assuming that a cat who appears in your yard looking for food is homeless, try to find out whether the cat belongs somewhere else. Check for a collar with an ID tag, and if possible, take a few pictures and post them to social media, asking local friends to check around and see if anyone's missing a cat.

Gain their trust: Stray cats can be skittish and scared of people, especially if they're feral. If your stray cat isn't immediately friendly and approachable, be prepared to have a lot of patience while you gain their trust. The best way to do this is to leave food out for them and be present, at a distance, when they come to eat. Then you can move closer over a period of days or even weeks. For example, you might place food at the far end of your yard while sitting on the porch, and then slowly move the food dish closer to your house each day. The goal is to coax the cat either onto the closed porch or inside the house while building enough trust that the cat will let you handle them.

Build up supplies: Once you decide to bring a stray cat into your home, you should start getting supplies for them to live with you. Be sure to have, at minimum, a litter box, food and water dishes, and plenty of food and litter on hand. You may also want to pick up some toys and cat furniture, such as beds and scratching posts. You'll also need a cat carrier for the most important step in adopting a stray cat, which is…

Get to the vet ASAP: When bringing in a stray cat, it's critical to bring them to a veterinarian as soon as possible, especially if you already have cats in the house. You need to make sure the cat is healthy and in good physical shape, as strays and feral cats are at higher risk for illness and injury. You'll also want to bring the cat up to date on any vaccinations they require, find out their approximate age, and scan for a microchip in case the cat is a runaway with an owner who's looking for them. With a clean bill of health and some mutual trust, you can bring your stray cat home (assuming they don't belong to anyone else) and start enjoying each other's company.

Consider Fostering First: Help Cats in Need While You Help Yourself

If you're not sure exactly how you plan to obtain a cat, or if you've never owned a cat and want to make sure the cat life is for you, one of the best things you can do is become a foster cat parent.

Cat fostering, typically done through pet rescue organizations, involves taking in cats and kittens on a transitional basis until they can be placed with forever homes. The goals of fostering are typically to alleviate overcrowding at shelters and rescues, to learn how individual cats will react in domestic situations, and to help cats who are feral, injured, sick, or victims of abuse to recover in a safe and loving environment while they become acclimated (or re-acclimated) to living in a home.

Cat fostering may be short-term or long-term, depending on the individual cat and how much care they need before they're ready to be adopted permanently. To foster cats, all you need is extra space and the willingness to dedicate your time and attention to helping cats become family members.

As a cat foster, you'll be able to help cats in need and reap all the benefits of having a cat around without the pressure of making an immediate commitment to a lifelong pet. You can find out what type of cat owner you are and discover the kinds of cats you'll be most compatible with, so when you're ready to adopt your forever cat, you'll have a better sense of what you're looking for.

Most cat foster parents find that the hardest part of fostering is giving up a cat to a new family after you've spent time nurturing and rehabilitating them. However, many adopt one (or more) of their fosters themselves—and if you have enough time and room in your house, you can continue to foster other cats even after you've adopted them permanently.

If you're interested in cat fostering, get in touch with a local pet rescue or pet shelter to find out whether they have a fostering program and ask how you can get involved. Fostering cats is an all-around rewarding experience for both cats and humans, and we doubt you'll ever regret the decision to give it a try.

In the next chapter, we're going to talk about training your cat for improved cat-human harmony... and for lots of fun with your furry companion!

CHAPTER 4

KITTY TRICKS: YOU CAN TRAIN YOUR CAT!

> "I had been told that the training procedure with cats was difficult. It's not. Mine had me trained in two days."
>
> – Bill Dana

There's a lot of misinformation surrounding the idea of training cats. Many people believe that cats simply aren't trainable and will never even try anything more complicated than litter box training – which, let's face it, most cats train themselves to do.

However, the idea that cats can't be trained at all is a misconception that you don't have to live with. Cats can definitely be trained to follow commands and perform tricks. They are curious, intelligent, and every bit as trainable as dogs – they simply operate with a different set of rules that you need to understand before you can effectively train them.

While each cat is unique, there are many areas where all cats exhibit similar behaviors. This includes the way they communicate and how they learn new skills. Since these are shared behaviors across the board, effective cat training methods will work with all types of cats.

Perhaps the most important thing to keep in mind is that cats have different motivations than dogs. Dog training may *seem* easier because most dogs' motivation is to make their owners happy. If a dog sees that something pleases you, they'll repeat the behavior to get that happy reaction.

In some cases, cats might also like making you happy. However, their main motivations are typically along the lines of "What's in it for me?" Dogs might enjoy getting rewarded for good behavior or performing a trick, but cats *expect* rewards – usually in the form of something tasty. This means the most effective training method for cats is positive reinforcement, which is the method we'll be discussing in this chapter.

As long as you keep cat motivations in mind, you can train your cat away from poor behaviors and even get them to perform some cool tricks. Just be prepared to make it worth their while!

What Do You Really Want to Teach Your Cat?

Before you embark on the adventure of training your cat, it's important to understand exactly what you want to teach them. If there are behavioral issues you're looking to correct, we'll cover those in the next chapter.

Positive reinforcement training can be used to train your cat in various ways. For example, you can teach your cat voice commands such as *sit, stay, come,* and even *fetch* (provided the fetching object in question is something your cat can physically handle). Your cat can learn to walk with a leash or ride comfortably in a car so that they can go on outings with you. There are even tricks that you can teach your cat, such as high-fiving and waving.

The thing to remember here is that training your cat requires time and patience. That's why it's important to decide what you want to teach your cat upfront, so you don't overwhelm yourself or your cat with too many tricks.

For instance, if your cat is strictly an indoor cat, your training focus may be on cute indoor tricks. If your cat goes outside sometimes, voice commands such as *come* and *stay* can be helpful, and leash training can help to ensure that your cat enjoys more of the outdoors safely. If you'd like to travel with your cat, you might teach them to enjoy car rides, be comfortable with carriers, and walk on a leash.

It's always good to have an agenda and your end goal in mind when you start training your cat. This way, you can see your progress, and you'll be less likely to give up if you hit a tough spot during the process.

What If My Cat Is Not Interested?

Maybe you've tried training your cat before, but they showed no interest in learning anything. Or maybe you'll come to notice, when you start training your cat, that they don't respond to your efforts. If this is the case, there are things you can do to figure out what's going wrong and steer your cat onto the training track.

Some things that may adversely affect your positive reinforcement training efforts include:

Stress/anxiety: Cats can get nervous under pressure, and if they don't want to do something at the moment, they simply won't. For this reason, it's important to keep your cat training sessions short and as stress-free as possible for both yourself and your cat. The more often your cat feels anxious during training, the less likely they will engage in future sessions.

Distractions: If there's something more interesting happening while you're trying to train your cat, their attention is likely to wander, and you'll end up getting nowhere. Try to create a quiet, calm environment for cat training, away from televisions, other pets or household members, and anything else that might pull your cat's attention away. You should also train your cat in a place where they don't have easy access to their food dishes, as they may be inclined to trot off for a snack rather than stick with the training.

The wrong treats: Just as cats have unique personalities, they also have unique tastes in treats, which are usually the primary motivating tool for training. If you're using treats as positive motivation and your cat seems to lose interest in earning one, it may be the case that the reward you're offering just isn't enough of a treat. Try using different flavors or types of treats (for example, moist or wet rather than crunchy treats) to find one that your cat goes wild for, and then keep the new treats on hand for future training sessions.

They're just not that into food: Some cats might simply never respond to treats as a reward, no matter how many different varieties you try. If this is the case with your cat, find out what they do want and offer it as a reward. If it's not food, it's often affection, so for these types of cats, give them plenty of praise and affection for responding to commands or performing a trick.

Your bond isn't strong yet: If you're trying to train a cat who's relatively new to your household, you may run into resistance that has nothing to do with the right treats or non-food motivation. It could be that your cat just doesn't really know you yet, and vice versa. Check out the last section of this chapter on bonding with your cat to see how you can strengthen that bond to the point where your cat wants to be trained.

How to Train Your Cat to Walk on a Leash

Leash training your cat can be challenging or frustrating, but it's also rewarding and worth the struggle. Once your cat is leash trained, you can both enjoy fresh air and outdoor walks together, explore the neighborhood, and get to know your surroundings. You could even meet some new friends – or just show off the awesomeness that is your cat.

As with any type of cat training, you should plan to take it slow, use positive reinforcement, and have a lot of patience with your cat. But by following these steps, you and your cat can reap the benefits of leash walking.

To start, you'll need the right equipment. Make sure you invest in a harness made specifically for cats because while a small dog harness may "fit" your cat, it's not designed to fit them properly. A dog harness may be uncomfortable for your cat, and they might even be able to slip out of it – which they'll definitely try to do if they're uncomfortable.

You'll also need a lightweight leash made from cloth or nylon. Chain leashes and retractable leashes aren't suitable for cats and could injure them.

Once you have the proper equipment, here's how to leash train your cat:

1. Help your cat get used to the harness by placing it on them indoors, without the leash attached. Give your cat a treat once the harness is on to encourage them to tolerate it. The first time they wear the harness, remove it immediately (and gently) after giving them a treat. Then, on subsequent days, start to gradually increase the length of time they wear the harness – while continuing to give treats when the harness is on – until your cat is comfortable with it.

2. When your cat is comfortable wearing a harness, it's time to get them used to a leash without tension. Again, this should be done indoors. Start by attaching the leash to the harness and giving your cat a treat, and then hold the leash loosely while you allow them to walk with you following behind them. After a few minutes, remove both the leash and the harness. As before, gradually increase the length of time you leave the leash connected until your cat is relaxed when walking with a loose leash.

3. The next step is to add a bit of leash tension to the process while still indoors. To do this, attach the leash to the harness and let your cat move around freely with the leash dragging. This will create a mild pull that your cat can get used to. Continue to do this each day and increase the time your cat walks with a dragging leash. Also, make sure to follow your cat around, even though you're not holding the leash. You should never leave a cat unsupervised while wearing a leash and harness.

4. Next, you'll combine the previous two steps as you start walking your cat indoors. With the harness on, attach the leash and hold it while following your cat. Once they've walked for a bit, try placing some slight tension on the leash to encourage your cat to change directions. Be sure to reward them with treats if they respond. If your cat doesn't move in the direction you're indicating, try luring them with treats by either holding the treat ahead of them in your fingers or dropping them on the floor in the corresponding direction. Repeat this step for slightly longer periods until your cat consistently responds to leash tension.

5. Now it's time to head outside! Choose a dry, mild day to start your outdoor adventures, as your cat isn't likely to enjoy going out during inclement weather. Gear up for your walk with treats to use for encouragement. Then, with the harness and leash on, walk your cat to the door you'll exit from and open it, then encourage them to go outside by tossing a treat out. If your cat hesitates or seems frightened, don't force them to go outside. Bring them back in, reward them with a treat, remove the harness, and try again another day. If they do head out, be sure to keep your walk short, especially in the beginning, since you'll want to make sure walking is a positive experience. From there, you can gradually increase the time you and your cat spend outdoors together.

Clicker Training: Cool Tricks Your Cat Can Learn

Using a clicker to train your cat may be much easier than you think. Most cats already respond to some type of audible signal, such as the sound of cat food being poured into a bowl, the whirr of a can opener, or the noise made by opening a pop-top can (even if it's soup instead of cat food).

Clicker training, therefore, is simply an extension of the response your cat already makes to signals. You can train your cat to learn that when they hear the clicker and perform an action, they'll get a reward, just like when they hear a can opener and come running, they get dinner.

To start with, you'll need a good supply of your cat's favorite treats and a clicker device. Clickers are inexpensive and available at most pet stores, department stores, and online. Alternatively, you can clicker train a cat by clicking your tongue – though you may want to invest in a clicker, especially if you want to teach your cat more than one trick.

Here are a few fun tricks you can teach your cat through clicker training:

Come: This is the easiest trick for a cat to learn. Start by positioning yourself where your cat can see you. Have a treat ready and show it to your cat, and be sure to click the clicker when they start approaching before giving them a treat. You can reinforce this trick by saying "come" or "here" after the click. After the first time, start increasing the distance from your cat. Soon enough, your cat will learn that when they hear a click, they get a treat, even if they're not in the room with you at the time.

Your cat will eventually come to you with just the verbal command if you speak it consistently. If you're planning to teach your cat more than one trick, it's best to use both the clicker and a verbal command so they can differentiate between tricks.

Sit (or sit pretty): For this trick, it's easiest to watch for the behavior you want and then reward it. When your cat is naturally sitting, simply click the clicker and give them a treat. This will help them associate sitting with the treat reward, and your cat will begin to sit in response to seeing you with a bag of treats. When your cat is sitting consistently, introduce the verbal command of "sit" or "sit pretty" along with the click, then give them a treat. You can phase out the clicker, if desired, and stick with the verbal command.

High five: To teach your cat this trick, you'll need to be on the same level as your cat. You can sit on the floor with them or position your cat on a table or chair. Start by holding a treat out in front of your cat's shoulder height. You'll need to make sure your cat reaches for the treat with a paw, so if they lean in to eat from your hand, pull the treat back a bit. When your cat stretches a paw out, touch it with your hand and click the clicker, then give the treat. You'll need to repeat this several times with the treat in your hand. When your cat consistently touches your hand for a treat, you can start offering just your hand with your palm out and add the voice command "high five" with the click. Then, give the treat after your cat touches your hand.

In the carrier: This trick is especially handy for vet trip days. It's also helpful to allow your cat to get used to being in the cat carrier so they don't automatically associate it with going to the vet. To start, leave the cat carrier open somewhere your cat can easily access and place a treat inside. When your cat goes into it, click the clicker to associate the sound with the treat. After a few times, you can add a voice command for "in the carrier" or "in the box." Eventually, you should close the carrier door after your cat jumps in and carry them around for a minute, then give them a treat after you let them out.

Hoop jumping: You can get your cat to jump through hoops for you! You should use a small hula hoop for this trick. Hold the hula hoop upright on the floor between you and your cat, and then hold up a treat on your side of the hoop. When your cat walks through, click the clicker and reward with the treat. You can start adding a verbal command like "hoop" the first time if you like. Once your cat is consistently walking through the hoop, stop using the clicker (but keep the treat!) and stick with the voice command. Then you can start gradually raising the hoop each time so that your cat jumps through it.

Keep in mind that, for all these tricks, it will take time for your cat to learn. Don't expect to repeat a trick several times in one day and have your cat trained. Long training sessions are likely to put your cat off doing tricks entirely. Instead, stick to just a few times a day and one trick at a time for training sessions.

How to Bond with Your Cat

New cats in the family need time to bond with you. You can help this process along without overwhelming your cat. If you don't already have one, establishing a bond between you and your cat is the best way to create a foundation for effective positive reinforcement training.

One way to do this, especially if your cat has just moved in and seems anxious, is to give them space. Many cats enjoy "vertical space," such as a cat tree, that allows them to perch up high and maintain a view of everything around them. Your cat might also like cardboard boxes, but to encourage safety and security, you should provide a box with entrance and exit holes cut out so your cat can escape if they need to.

Getting to know your cat is another way to increase the bond, and you can do this simply by observing them for a while. Pay attention to things like where they like to sleep, what they do when they're awake, and how they react to objects and situations. This observation will help you understand your cat's personality and determine what appeals to them as motivation.

Here are more steps to improve your cat-human bond:

- Wait for your cat to come to you, and encourage any bonding behaviors they offer, such as purring, kneading, rubbing, and head-butting.
- Give your cat space when they show signs of agitation.
- Treats, treats, and more treats – in general, tasty food is the surest way to a cat's heart.
- Pay attention to how your cat prefers to be petted, and continue the behaviors they like, such as head-scratching or face stroking.
- Make time for playing. If your cat seems mistrustful and won't play with a toy you're holding, consider starting with a laser pointer; they won't know you're holding it, but they'll get used to playing in the same room as you.

Now, let's move on to the next chapter, where we'll discuss several common cat behavior problems and how you can solve them gently and positively so that you and your cat can both enjoy hanging around together.

CHAPTER 5

LIVING THE CAT LIFE: CAT PROBLEMS AND HOW TO SOLVE THEM

> "Cats can work out mathematically the exact place to sit that will cause the most inconvenience."
>
> – Pam Brown

Though sometimes they might seem like it, cats are not actually angels. They sometimes struggle just like the rest of us, and as a result, their behavior isn't always perfect. The problem is that with people, we can just explain in words why a certain behavior is creating an issue. We don't have the same luxury with cats.

At first, communication with your cat might seem like a one-way street. You can learn to understand what the various sounds a cat makes mean, but no amount of practicing your meow repertoire will get them to understand what you're saying. So, we humans need to take a different approach to behavioral training.

Above all, you need to be gentle and patient with your cat. Too often, the idea that cats can't be trained out of unwanted behaviors leads to pets being surrendered at shelters or rescues. Keep in mind that they may make mistakes along the way – not out of any maliciousness or particular desire. Cats simply follow their instincts.

If you can't even stomach the idea of a cat scratching your furniture or walls, please don't get a cat. However, if you're willing to suffer a few bumps along the road to a peaceful, happy cat-human existence, read on to learn about solving common behavior issues with your cat.

Why Playing with Your Cat Is Essential

Wild cats have a simple rhythm to their lives. It goes something like this: Hunt, catch, kill, eat, groom, sleep, repeat. You may notice that there's no "play" in there. Wild cats engage in play, but only after their needs are met. This means playtime is erratic, depending on whether or not they've hunted enough to fill their bellies.

Cats who live with humans, on the other hand, can skip over the hunt-catch-kill portion of cat life and move straight to eating. However, they still retain the instinct to engage in this rhythm. If a cat is not hunting, it's easy for boredom to move into the space this instinct should occupy. This boredom can lead to destruction, as your cat, in the absence of prey, decides to hunt, catch, and kill something else – like your yarn stash, paper towel roll, shoes, or any other object that's accessible and doesn't run away.

This is where playing with your cat comes in. Playtime helps your cat expend the energy they would have otherwise used to hunt, so they can spend the rest of their time eating, grooming, and sleeping without the need to destroy "prey."

It's best to set aside ten minutes or so, around three times a day, to play with your cat using interactive objects like string toys, wands, or laser pointers. You should also consider cat enrichment toys like food puzzles or cat trees with built-in toys so your cat can amuse themselves when you're not available – without resorting to "hunting" your possessions.

Step One in Solving Behavioral Issues: Is Your Cat Spayed/Neutered?

If your cat engages in problematic behaviors, you should consider whether this problem would be solved by having them spayed or neutered. Some instinctive behaviors are mainly prevalent for intact (un-spayed or unneutered) cats – as they're purely the result of shifting hormones – and can be eased by having your cat fixed. These behaviors include:

Aggression. If your intact female cat seems to have a split personality, where she loves you to pieces one moment and tries to claw you to death the next, this can be due to her hormone cycle. Hormones cause mood swings, just like in human females. Intact male cats might also become aggressive due to hormones, but this emotion is usually reserved for other male cats – either as a territorial dispute or in competition for a female in heat.

Escaping. Intact female cats will try to flee the house when they're in heat, while intact males tend to make a break for it when there's a female outside looking for attention. In either case, having your cat fixed can improve their safety and temperament by reducing their urge to bolt.

Bathroom issues. You've probably heard of spraying, which is a territorial behavior among intact male cats that involves marking their "property" with concentrated urine – their property being your home, not just the litter box. Additionally, both male and female intact cats may use feces as hormonal scent markers and deposit them around the house in unexpected places.

Vocalization. For the most part, a cat's meow is adorable–except when it's loud, aggressive, and happens in the middle of the night. Cats are usually most active from dusk until the early morning hours, and intact females in heat tend to look for love at night. This is also when intact males make loud vocalizations – often responding to an intact female.

If your intact cat displays these behaviors, it's a good idea to talk to your vet about getting them spayed or neutered.

Common Behavior Problems in Cats

Here are some of the most common behavior problems you might see in cats and how you can approach and conquer them to make you and your cat happier and more relaxed.

Excessive scratching: There may be several reasons why your cat scratches furniture or walls. One is that scratching is instinctual behavior. Cats' claws can get overgrown and uncomfortable if they don't wear them down through scratching. Other reasons for this behavior include:

- ✧ Boredom or attention-seeking
- ✧ Marking their territory
- ✧ The presence of pests, such as mice in the walls (which your cat can hear, even if you can't)

To curb this behavior, make sure your cat's claws are regularly trimmed to a suitable length. If you're not sure what length is suitable, ask your vet for advice, or you can bring your cat to a groomer for nail trimming sessions.

Also, make sure you provide at least one scratching surface, preferably more than one, that your cat can access. Consider scratching posts and wall-mounted scratch pads. You might also want to offer a horizontal scratching surface such as a scratch pad or ramp to see which your cat prefers. Make sure your cat is getting enough attention and playtime to alleviate boredom, as well.

If the scratching is territorial (most common in multi-cat households), encourage your cat to rub their scent on the walls rather than scratching. You can do this by gently removing your cat when they scratch at walls and petting them for encouragement. There are also cat pheromone products such as sprays and wipes that you can use on your walls to discourage scratching.

And of course, you'll want to ensure that there are no pests in your walls, in case that is the reason for your cat's scratching.

Nuisance behaviors: Common so-called nuisance behaviors in cats can include eating house plants, excessive vocalization, jumping on tables or counters, and biting or scratching during play. If your cat...

- ✧ *Eats your plants*: Plant eating is a natural behavior for cats, and many will chew on any leafy greens they can find. To stop this, first make sure to remove any toxic plants to cats from your home, such as peace lilies, aloe vera, poinsettias, hydrangea, and mistletoe. If you're not sure whether you have toxic plants, ask your vet or do some research. The next step is to relocate your house plants to an area where your cat can't access them. Finally, pick up some pots of cat grass (you can usually find this in your local pet store) and place them around the house so your cat can chew away without destroying other plants.

- *Vocalizes excessively*: If your fixed cat is constantly making noise, chances are it's a cry for attention, and they need more playtime and affection. You can help alleviate this by providing enrichment activities that your cat can use, such as food-dispensing toys. Also, keep in mind that by rewarding your cat with attention when they cry for it, you're reinforcing the behavior – so try to engage them in play or enrichment activities *before* they start to complain.

- *Jumps on tables/counters*: Cats love to perch in high places. Again, this instinctual behavior helps them remain alert to their surroundings and avoid danger. If your cat is a counter-jumper, you can discourage this by placing double-sided tape on the surfaces they jump to but make sure you're offering an alternative high perch, such as a tall cat tree, cat shelves, or a cat condo, so they have a safe place to hang out and sleep.

- *Bites or scratches while playing:* To change this behavior, supply your cat with lots of toys. You should never use your hands, feet, or other body parts to play with your cat, as this will reinforce that biting or scratching is okay (remember, playtime is a substitute for hunt-catch-kill). Instead, opt for interactive toys like cat wands, jingle or catnip balls, laser lights, or toy mice. If your cat does bite or scratch, don't scold or shout at them; this will only scare them and make them even more defensive. Instead, use your free hand to make distracting noises, such as slapping the floor so your cat will release you, then grab a toy to continue playing with a redirected target.

Anxiety: An anxious cat will often display unwanted behavior, but you *definitely* shouldn't hold it against them. Signs of anxiety in cats can include withdrawal and hiding, aggressive posturing and vocalization, destructive behavior, excessive sleeping, excessive grooming, and/or going outside the litter box, among others.

Soothing an anxious cat requires time and patience. You'll need to identify the source of your cat's anxiety, then work toward removing anxiety triggers from their environment and providing positive alternate options.

Pay attention to what's happening when your cat exhibits anxious behavior – is it in response to loud noise? Are they bothered by another cat in the household? Do they hide in high places, such as top shelves in closets or pantries?

Once you've learned what is making your cat anxious, take steps toward giving them safe, positive options. If they're hiding or having problems with another cat, give them a space that's all their own, such as a cat tree or condo that's separate from communal cat furniture. If loud noises frighten them, be sure to give them extra attention during or after loud disturbances, so they understand that they're safe.

My cat is a killer: Excessive hunting can become an issue in some cases, especially if your cat is an indoor/outdoor cat. If your cat is allowed outdoors, you may find that they often bring back dead "treasures" and deposit them in the house. There are a few theories about why cats do this

– your cat may be trying to provide for you, or they may simply not want to eat in the same place where they hunted.

Whatever the case, hunting prey is instinctual behavior that can only be stopped by not allowing your cat outdoors (unless, of course, the prey enters your home). However, your cat may not be happy cooped up in the house all the time.

So, while you cannot stop your outdoor cat from hunting, you can help to reduce the amount of slain prey. You can give them a collar with a bell so the jingling alerts small animals before your cat can pounce. Or you can compromise by keeping your cat indoors during the times when their most successful hunts happen and letting them out at times when they don't tend to bring back their kills.

My cat is fat: Fat cats are cute, but obesity can cause health problems for your cat. Excess weight gain happens most often after spaying or neutering, as having your cat fixed tends to derail some of the behaviors that expend energy. So, what should you do if your cat is fat?

First, make sure that your cat actually is "too" fat. It can be hard to make that call, especially from breed to breed, as different cat breeds have different body shapes and fat distribution. It's best to check with your veterinarian to determine whether your cat is obese.

If your vet confirms that your cat is obese, they can help you formulate a weight loss plan for your cat that meets their nutritional needs. Do not try to "put your cat on a diet" without expert guidance, as this can lead to malnourishment and escalating health problems.

You can also work on increasing your cat's activity levels to help them shed excess weight. Engage your cat in play more often, and provide a wider selection of enrichment toys to encourage them to stay active.

My cat seems bored: Does your cat lie around the house, looking pitiful or exasperated? This could be a sign of boredom, but it's not the only one. Indications that your cat may be bored include:

- Repetitive behaviors like excessive vocalizing or over-grooming
- Unusually long periods of inactivity
- Overeating
- Destructive behaviors
- Chasing, annoying, or terrorizing other household pets

What can you do to help alleviate your cat's boredom? Of course, the obvious answer is to give them something to do in the form of playtime or providing more toys that they can amuse themselves with. Other possibilities include letting them "outside" on an enclosed porch or leash-training them so you can take them for short walks so they can experience a new environment, providing your "only cat" with a new feline companion to keep them company, or spending more time together that doesn't involve playing, such as brushing, cuddling, or napping.

Why Does My Cat…?

Some common cat behaviors may seem mysterious, but there's often a known reason behind them. So, why does your cat…

…*get the zoomies?*

The zoomies – those times when your cat runs around the house in seemingly aimless patterns, possibly putting on a cat-robatic show complete with leaps and flips – are usually your cat's attempt to release pent-up energy. Unfortunately, most cases of the zoomies seem to occur at night while you're trying to sleep. To avoid this, make sure you're encouraging activity throughout the day, so your cat isn't conserving all the fun for the wee hours.

…*sleep all the time?*

The "lazy cat" stereotype comes from the amount of time cats spend sleeping, which is considerably more than humans. Most cats get an average of 15 hours of sleep a day, with some spending up to 20 out of every 24 hours in snooze-ville. Moreover, cats are crepuscular (not nocturnal, as many believe), which means they're most active at dusk and dawn (twilight).

This cat cycle is very different from the typical human diurnal (active during the day) rhythm, so your cat's penchant for sleeping until the sun goes down may cause some household disruptions. However, the good news is that cats are both sociable and adaptable. With a bit of practice, you can help your cat become more active throughout the day so you can both sleep at night.

...chatter to the birds?

Not all cats do this, but you'll know it if yours does. Chattering behavior is when your cat sits at the window, rapidly clicking or vibrating their jaw while making a distinct noise that sounds like a bird call. Usually, your cat sees a bird on the other side of the window when they make this sound.

No one is one hundred percent certain why cats chatter at birds (or squirrels or chipmunks or any small animal that might be tasty). Theories about this behavior include:

- Chattering sounds from your cat are an attempt to copy the bird sounds and draw the feathered snack closer so they can pounce.
- Your cat mimics the "killing bite" that they would apply to prey if only the prey were in their claws instead of through the impenetrable glass.
- The cat is incredibly frustrated that their potential prey is so close yet so far away.
- Your cat is very excited to discover a new feathered friend and wants to communicate.

Whatever the reason behind cat chattering, it's not harmful or worrisome for your cat, and it's adorable to watch.

...knead and drool on me?

If your cat kneads you by pushing their paws in and out against you, this is a sign that your cat trusts you and feels comfortable and secure in your presence. This instinctual behavior is what kittens do while nursing. It's also believed that some wild cats knead the ground when they're about to go to sleep to smooth down foliage, so this could be a prelude to your cat snuggling up for a snooze on their favorite human pillow.

However, kneading and drooling might also be signs of a health problem. Stress and anxiety in cats can lead to excessive drooling. Your cat may also drool if suffering from an oral or dental condition. If your cat is kneading/drooling and showing signs of discomfort such as excessive grooming or vocalizations, you should discuss this with your vet.

...think I need grooming?

Cats groom with their tongues. If your cat seems to enjoy licking you, especially if they lick your hair, they may be grooming you. It's a sign of affection and acceptance.

Some cats may knead your head while you're lying down, but this isn't exactly grooming. Rather, it's a signal that your cat is happy and/or wants your attention. Among cats, grooming is only done with tongues.

This doesn't mean that your cat believes you are just another cat. By grooming you, your cat is signifying a strong relationship through cat-friendly behaviors.

...headbutt me?

You may receive the occasional, or not so occasional, headbutt from your cat. This bonk often comes when you're not expecting it and might feel insistent (although it certainly doesn't hurt!). Why the headbutting? Cats have scent glands on their cheeks, foreheads, and chins that contain pheromones – a kind of scent communication that animals can detect but people can't. Headbutting deposits these pheromones on your skin from the scent glands behind their ears.

There may be a few reasons for headbutting behavior. Most likely, your cat is marking you as a bonding activity, claiming you as "their people." A headbutt may also be a self-soothing behavior or a way to seek attention, but overall, they want to make sure you smell like them. This is a very good sign for bonding with your cat.

...want to sleep on my laptop?

If you have both a cat and a laptop in your house, you probably already know that laptops attract cats like honey attracts flies – especially if you happen to be working on the laptop in question. Why does your kitty feel compelled to camp out on your keyboard while you're working?

There are two main reasons for this behavior. One is that your cat wants to hang around wherever you are, which happens to be on your laptop. Another is for the heat your perfectly cat-sized device generates. You may have noticed that when cats choose a window to sleep near, they prefer one where the sun is streaming in. Cats love to be warm, and curling up on your laptop keyboard is like having a catnap in the sunshine.

If you'd like to discourage this behavior, consider getting an inexpensive heating pad to keep nearby, along with a comfy towel or blanket. When kitty comes over to investigate while you're working on your laptop, turn the heating pad on, place the towel or blanket over it, and relocate your cat to the new warm spot, with plenty of encouragement to stay and curl up there. Eventually, your cat should switch to the heating pad.

...hate my partner/spouse?

Not all cats exhibit this type of behavior, but it can happen with some cats, especially those who weren't well socialized as kittens. They may choose you as their person and bond with you but fail to bond with other adult humans in the household. Or, if the cat was there first and you introduce a new partner to the house, they might see this new human as a threat and fear them.

Often, the best way to help your cat overcome this type of social barrier may seem counterintuitive: You should try inviting more people over to visit. Cats are highly adaptable, but they need time to get used to changes in their environment. So, if you have strangers in the house more often, your cat will come to expect the presence of "new people" – even if they are never overjoyed about it – and you'll be able to curb any aggressive behavior.

Another possible reason for aggression toward your partner, although less common, is that a new partner may be abusing your cat when you're not watching. If your cat seems especially anxious, frightened, or angry around your partner, try discussing their feelings toward your cat. You may find out they have little regard for your pet... in which case, stand your ground and side with your cat since they were there first.

...want to play at 4 a.m.?

As mentioned earlier, cats are crepuscular (most active at twilight). Many cats are still guided by instincts, and the wee morning hours are when their prey is most active. This leads them to sleep most of the day to conserve their energy for night hunts.

For household cats, playtime can replace hunting time and help cats expend energy. However, if your cat is used to playing to burn off the hunting stamina they've built up, they might seek you out in the middle of the night, looking for their favorite string toy to attack.

One way to help shift your cat's body clock back a few hours is to make your evening playtime longer and closer to your bedtime. This will allow your cat to burn through energy, so they're tired enough to sleep at night.

You can also make sure you're providing toys that your cat can rely on to amuse themselves when you're not available.

To reinforce the idea that you're not going to get up in the middle of the night for playtime, be sure that you don't respond if your cat tries to wake you. Eventually, they'll realize that late-night play sessions are off the table and find a way to amuse themselves.

What you *don't* want to do is "punish" your cat for nocturnal activity. This will only make them anxious and fray the cat-owner bond, which may make them more aggressive toward you (and far less trainable).

...get so greedy?

Does your cat seem to double as a food vacuum? Some cats may look like they're eating far more than they need, to the point where they not only finish all their food but end up begging for more, and they may even try to steal any human food they can reach. They might also eat very quickly as if they're worried the food might vanish. The most likely reasons your cat may seem "greedy" are:

- ✧ Instinct: Wild cats who hunt for their food tend to gulp it down quickly, both because they're worried that another predator might make a try for it and they're not sure how long it will be until their next meal. If your cat is acting on instinct and scarfing their food down, they're likely to slow this behavior once they realize that their next meals will always be supplied.

- ✧ Nutrition deficiency: If your cat seems to be eating a lot and seeking out other food beyond what's in their bowl, they may be lacking in some necessary nutrients. In this case, consider consulting your vet to make sure your cat's food is meeting their dietary needs.

- Medical issues: Some illnesses, including parasites, diabetes, and hyperthyroidism, can cause increased appetite in cats. Again, you'll want to consult with your veterinarian to rule out this possibility.

...hate closed doors?

You enter the bedroom or the bathroom, close the door, and before long, there's a pitiful meow from the other side or a little paw sticking under the door. Why does your cat freak out in the presence of closed doors?

There could be a few reasons for this. It may simply be normal cat curiosity, wanting to know what they're missing out on. If they're on the inside of a closed door, such as shut in a room, they probably feel trapped. They may have separation anxiety when they can't see you, or they could have learned that if they make noise outside a door, you'll open it.

While not a harmful behavior, you may want to encourage your cat not to be anxious about closed doors. You can do this by making your cat's own "space" as fun and comfortable as possible, so they don't view closed doors as punishment or entrapment. You can also spend time in the room with your cat while the door is closed to help them see that a closed door isn't a way to shut them off from you.

...act so clingy/needy?

If your cat seems unable to exist without being close to you at all times, you might have a clingy cat. Clinginess manifests in a cat who follows you around (including to the bathroom), constantly meowing or demanding your attention, and rubbing against you or sulking when you're about to leave the house. Clingy cats might also refuse to eat unless you're home and may exhibit destructive behaviors or make messes outside the litter box.

Sometimes a clingy cat may be bored and need more playtime or stimulation. Clinginess might also occur in cats who have been separated from their mothers too soon. In other cases, a change in routine or an illness may bring about clingy behavior. Or, your kitty may simply be spoiled.

If your cat's clinginess is disruptive, the first thing you need to do is identify the cause of the behavior. Make sure to schedule plenty of playtime and provide toys to keep them busy while you're away. If your "only cat" is clingy and possibly spoiled, consider getting a second cat for companionship. Finally, speak with your vet – especially if clingy behavior is not normal for your cat – to rule out any medical complications.

...hate going to the vet?

The struggle of getting a cat to the vet for a visit is nearly universal. Unless your cat is incredibly laid-back and easygoing, chances are it's going to be a fight to bring them to the vet's office, to sit in the waiting room, to have examinations, and whatever else they need in terms of healthcare and finally to bring them home.

Why do cats hate vets as much as dogs hate mail carriers? For the most part, it's because the entire experience from start to finish is unfamiliar, and cats thrive on consistency and routine. A massive disruption in their day-to-day life is bound to put them on edge.

Furthermore, if you're apprehensive about taking your cat to the vet, your cat will sense your mood and react accordingly by reflecting even more anxiety over the ordeal.

Some things you can do to try and ease veterinary visits for your feline family member include:

- ✧ Remain positive about the trip, so that you can transfer some of your relaxed mood to your cat.

- ✧ Train your cat to be comfortable traveling in a carrier, as discussed in a previous chapter.

- ✧ If you have a kitten or young cat, be sure they get plenty of socialization, so they're more acclimated to touch when they travel to meet strange new humans.

- ✧ Practice occasional car rides that don't involve going to the vet (with your cat in a carrier), so they're more used to the motions of a moving vehicle.

- ✧ See if there's a cats-only veterinary clinic near you or one with a separate waiting room for cats and dogs if your cat gets skittish around animals who are larger than them.

- ✧ Consider using a calming aid like pheromone wipes or sprays on the cat carrier and the blanket you use inside to help your cat relax during the trip.

- ✧ If your cat is especially anxious or fearful, try calling ahead to the vet to see if there are any special arrangements that can be made to accommodate your petrified kitty.

...get so picky about their food?

Most cats dislike change, and the food they prefer to eat is no exception. If your cat has just joined your household and doesn't seem interested in the food you're offering, try to find out what brand and flavor they had been eating in their previous living situation and offer that.

For cats who have suddenly stopped eating food they usually enjoy, they may be looking for a change. While cats prefer consistency, they can get tired of eating the same food all the time, just like people can. Consider switching to a raw food diet for your cat instead of commercial cat food.

...never finish the food in their bowl?

Does your cat's food bowl never seem to empty itself? Cats are fairly good at self-regulating and, for the most part, will stop eating when they're full (unless the food is particularly tasty to them, in which case they might overindulge). So, it's unnecessary to assume that a partially full food bowl means your cat is starving themselves.

Another reason your cat may not empty their bowl that many cat owners aren't aware of has to do with their whiskers. If your cat consistently eats the food from the center of the bowl but leaves a ring around the outer edge that never gets touched, it's likely because their whiskers are extremely sensitive. Depending on the breed and each cat's physique, it may be painful when their whiskers press down on the sides of the bowl as they try to eat the food that's further inside, so they just leave that outer ring untouched and then complain that their dish is "empty."

If your cat's eating pattern resembles this, you can either get them a shallower food bowl or raise the bowl off the surface it's usually on so your cat can be in a less painful position to eat all the food. For cats with sensitive whiskers, a good option may be to serve their food on a plate rather than in a bowl.

...hate being petted/picked up?

Cuddling with a kitty can be one of the best perks of cat ownership... but what if your cat hates being held or petted? If your cat is not particularly affectionate, it may be because of your kitty:

- ✧ Wasn't socialized well as a kitten
- ✧ Has a history of trauma involving humans

- ✧ May be in pain or sick (for cats who are usually all snuggles but suddenly resist affection)
- ✧ Could instinctually perceive petting or picking up as a threat to their safety

In most of these cases, after you rule out illness, time and patience is the only way to achieve snuggly satisfaction. Trying to force your cat to accept physical affection will only backfire and make them less likely to welcome your touch. Instead, focus on strengthening the bond between you and your cat by spending time with them, engaging in play, and even teaching them tricks. It'll be all the more rewarding when your cat finally relaxes into a cuddle with you.

Challenging behaviors in your cat can be frustrating, but with patience and understanding, you can move quickly toward changing those behaviors for the better – with your cat's full cooperation. Next up, we'll to talk litter boxes – how to solve problems surrounding them, the best boxes and litter types for you and your cat, and more.

CHAPTER 6

BATHROOM BLUES: SOLVING COMMON LITTER BOX ISSUES

> "His movements could be called cat-like, except that he did not stop to spray urine up against things."
>
> – Terry Pratchett

Aside from litter training your cat, having the right litter box – and the right litter – is important for a happy and harmonious cat-human household. These issues are among the most stressful that cat owners can have. Litter boxes are smelly, they're not fun to clean, and if your cat stops using the litter box for whatever reason, the smells and the messes are even worse. In this chapter, we'll go over common bathroom problems that cats may have and help you figure out the best litter box and type of litter for your cat.

Does Your Kitty Have Litter Issues?

It can be a major problem when your previously well-litter-trained cat starts going outside the box... literally. Urinary issues in cats are very common. Several illnesses can cause urinary problems, resulting in your cat peeing outside the litter box. These include:

- *Urinary tract infections (UTIs):* This condition is more likely to affect older cats, although rarely, young cats may get UTIs. The infection causes swelling in the urinary tract, making it painful for your kitty to pee. UTIs must be treated with antibiotics.

- *Bladder stones:* This illness occurs when stones develop in the bladder, causing irritation and sometimes blockage, depending on the size of the stones. Your vet can diagnose bladder stones with X-rays. A special diet can help your cat dissolve smaller stones, but your cat may need surgery if there are large stones. Cats often develop UTIs in conjunction with bladder stones, so they may also need antibiotics.

- *Bladder inflammation:* Medically termed *idiopathic cystitis*, this condition is when the bladder becomes inflamed for unknown reasons. If your cat suffers from an irritated bladder, diet and environmental changes can help. Your vet may also prescribe pain medication.

- *Metabolic diseases:* There are a few metabolic diseases in cats that can affect urination, including liver disease, chronic kidney disease, diabetes, and thyroid issues. One of the possible symptoms of metabolic disease is increased thirst, so if your cat is drinking more water than usual or you need to clean the litter box more often, it's a good idea to discuss this with your vet.

Behavioral Problems and Litter Box Issues

If your cat's bathroom blues are not medical, the problems are likely behavioral. The most common scenario here is that your cat simply doesn't like something about the litter box; it may be too dirty, too small, covered/not covered (depending on your cat's preferences), too high, or too low. Your cat might also not like the litter itself; they may not like the smell, the feel, or the composition of the litter.

Other behavioral possibilities might be:

- ✧ Your cat is stressed out by something in the home. If there's a new pet in the household, your cat may pee outside the box to mark their territory (this is a common behavior for intact males). The same goes for having a new human in the house.

- ✧ The spot where your cat pees is one where they've peed before, and the smell lingers. Cats tend to urinate in the same places, so if it already smells like their own urine, they'll continue to go there. Be sure to thoroughly clean any areas where your cat has gone outside the box to prevent this.

- ✧ Your cat had a traumatic experience in the litter box, whether they are (or were) in pain due to a medical condition or they were startled by a person or another pet while trying to use the litter box. If this is the reason for litter box avoidance, your cat may choose to pee in the bathtub instead.

What Type of Litter Box Should You Get?

As with most cat-related things, the best type of litter box for your household depends on your cat (or cats). The number of litter boxes is also important; the general rule is that you should have at least one more litter box than you have cats. If you're an "only" cat parent, provide two litter boxes; if you have two cats, set up three litter boxes; and so forth. Giving your kitty choices for bathroom time helps to ensure against accidents. And for multi-cat households, multiple litter boxes are a must.

If you've shopped around for litter boxes, you may have noticed that pet parents are spoiled for choice. There are tons of different litter boxes available, from the traditional rectangular tray you can pick up for about five bucks to "smart" self-cleaning models that cost hundreds of dollars. How do you know which one is right for you? Some guidelines for choosing a litter box include:

The size of your cat: Litter boxes need to be roomy enough for your cat to dig around and get comfortable while using it, with enough space to avoid going in the same spot twice between scooping. The length of your cat's litter box should be at least the length of your cat from nose to tail, and the width should be at least as big as your cat without their tail extended. This goes for any style of litter box, including enclosed boxes.

Accessibility: How your cat will enter the litter box is also an important determination. For small kittens and older cats with less mobility, you'll need at least one low entrance for them to use. Three-sided litter boxes with a scoop entrance on the fourth side are usually best for kittens and older cats. You can also try covered boxes with low entrances.

Litter box height: Aside from accessibility concerns (for example, a standard or deep rectangular litter box may be too high for kittens or cats with mobility issues), the best height for a litter box depends on your cat's bathroom habits. If your cat is fastidious about using the bathroom and doesn't make much of a mess outside the box, a standard large-box wall height of around 5 to 7 inches should be sufficient. For cats who tend to kick litter out of the box, spray across the edges, or simply have bad aim, you may want a taller box with wall heights of 8 to 12 inches and a lowered or scoop entrance on one side.

Covered or uncovered? It is tempting to choose a covered litter box simply because it's better at hiding the smell, but in this case, it's important to let your cat make the decision over whether they prefer a covered or uncovered box. Some cats are happy to use a covered box. Others can tolerate the more concentrated smell inside a covered litter box and will refuse to use it.

If you'd like to try a covered litter box, be sure to have both a covered and uncovered option available so you can learn your cat's preferences. Additionally, covered litter boxes must be scooped a minimum of once daily because once the odors build-up, your cat will be reluctant to use it and may seek another, less litter-filled place to relieve themselves.

Self-cleaning litter boxes: You may have seen the commercial where the husband and wife are competing for who gets to clean the litter box, and the wife is excited to win the chore – because the self-cleaning litter box does all the work, removing clumps and waste, so you only have to empty a disposal compartment once in a while. It's easy to see the appeal of never having to scoop cat litter manually. However, despite the ease of maintenance, a self-cleaning litter box may not be the right choice. Before deciding, you should consider the pros and cons of these types of litter boxes.

Pros of self-cleaning litter boxes:

- ✧ No daily litter scooping required
- ✧ The odor around the litter box is greatly reduced and sometimes non-existent
- ✧ Occasional, easy waste disposal by emptying the collection compartment

Cons of self-cleaning litter boxes:

- Far more expensive than regular litter boxes, as they may cost anywhere from around $100 to $500 depending on the model
- Most require special cat litter (that your cat may not like) and disposable trays at extra cost
- The movement of the mechanism inside a self-cleaning litter box may be startling to your cat and bring about litter box avoidance behavior
- Depending on the model, some cleaning cycles for self-cleaning litter boxes are loud enough to cause disturbances and may even wake you up if your cat uses the box in the middle of the night

One final tip for choosing the right litter box for your cat: If you've tried several different litter box types and your cat doesn't seem to like any of them, consider placing the box in different rooms of the house. Litter box location matters, especially for cats who may struggle with anxiety and need a quiet, low-traffic area to do their business.

Cat Litter: The Good, the Bad, and the Ugly

Just as there are many types of litter boxes, you'll find plenty of cat litter varieties to choose from. The cost, ease of use, and safety of each type varies, so it's important to understand what's involved with each one.

Clay cat litter is the cheapest, most widely available standard option. It is non-clumping, so if you use it, your cat's litter box will need a complete litter replacement more often – a minimum of twice a week. Many clay cat litters generate dust, especially when first filling the litter box; this dust can also cloud up while your cat is digging. Depending on the ingredients used in the litter, the dust could be harmful – such as those that contain quartz silica, which is a known carcinogen.

Clumping cat litter, although slightly more expensive than clay, is the most commonly used type. The litter forms clumps when your cat urinates and dries out bowel movements, allowing you to remove the waste with a litter scoop. Complete litter box changes still need to be done, but not as often as with clay litter. With clumping litter, the litter box should be scooped out daily and completely changed at least once a month.

There are a few important things to know here. First, sodium bentonite – the agent that causes the litter to clump – expands up to 18 times its size when wet. This means you can't flush clumps down your toilet, as it could damage your drainage pipes. Additionally, if your cat ingests clumping litter, it may swell in their intestines and cause health problems. Finally, many types of clumping litter are scented with fragrances. Although it can help with litter box odor, some cats dislike artificial scents and refuse to use the litter box.

Silica cat litter is made from the same material that often comes in small packets of beads placed into products like shoes and dry foods to keep moisture away, the little packages that say DO NOT EAT on them. Although silica dust may be harmful, this type of litter is dust-free and highly absorbent. When using silica litter, you'll need to scoop out solid waste daily and stir the crystals around in the box, so no single area gets too saturated. You'll also completely change the litter once a month.

Some drawbacks to silica litter are that, like clumping litter, it may be scented. Some cats also object to the texture of silica litter, as it's very different from clay and clumping litter with much larger, solid grains. You may also get pools of urine at the bottom of the litter box if the crystals have been fully saturated.

Natural cat litter, as the name suggests, is made with natural ingredients – typically pine, wood, wheat, or corn. There are several different texture options for natural litter, including pellets, paper, sawdust, and sand. Some natural litter is even made from orange peels. Generally, natural cat litter tends to be more expensive than other types. It is scoopable since the materials clump naturally and must be changed every two to four weeks, depending on the texture of the materials used and how quickly your cat fills the box.

If you want to go for natural litter, you may need to experiment with the various textures before finding one that your cat tolerates. One advantage of this litter type is that it's completely non-toxic and won't harm your cat if they ingest any while grooming or decide to nibble on some litter.

Why Pine Pellets Are Purr-fect for the Litter Box

In our experience, pine pellet litter is the best in terms of health, performance, and environmental friendliness, with the fewest drawbacks. Some potential downsides to pine pellets include cost and cat preferences. In general, pine pellet cat litter is more expensive than clumping litter, since you'll need to fully change the litter box more often. As for preference, some cats don't like the paw-feel of pellets or find it difficult to dig into, preventing them from using it.

However, if your cat is fine with pine, there are several great advantages:

- ✧ Pine litter is completely natural, non-toxic, and virtually dust-free, so it won't cause health issues for your cat.

- Because it's made with natural materials, it's biodegradable and environmentally friendly.

- The mild natural scent of pine helps to camouflage urine odors without overwhelming your cat's sensitive nose. It doesn't do much to cover the smell of solid waste, but this odor fades naturally when the waste dries and doesn't linger like urine.

- Pine cat litter is lightweight, scoopable, and flushable, so it's easier to dispose of waste.

- It has natural antimicrobial properties that help keep the litter box free of bacteria between emptying and cleaning cycles.

- While pine litter must be replaced more often than clumping litter, it can last for up to a month between changes with daily scooping, which is longer than other natural litters and considerably longer than clay.

It may require a bit of experimentation in the beginning, but finding the right combination of litter box and cat litter for your cat will help you solve the majority of any bathroom issues that may arise in your household.

Speaking of beginnings, in the next chapter, we will discuss bringing a new cat or kitten into the house, with helpful information for first-time cat owners and those who are adding a new cat to the existing mix.

CHAPTER 7

WELCOME HOME, KITTY: A GUIDE FOR BRINGING YOUR NEW PET INTO YOUR HOUSEHOLD

> "It is a truth universally acknowledged that a man in possession of a warm house and a well-stocked fridge must be in want of a cat."
>
> – Heather Hacking

You've decided to invite a cat into your life. We think that's a great idea! When you're bringing a new cat into your home, whether it's a kitten or a cat from a shelter or rescue, there are many things you should do to prepare for enriching your life with the addition of a cat.

In this chapter, we'll talk about how to kick things off on the right paw, so the transition is as smooth as possible for both you and your cat.

Rescue vs. Shelter: What's the Difference?

You may already know where you're going to get your cat. Perhaps you've agreed to take in a cat for a friend or family who can no longer care for them, or maybe someone you know is having kittens and cannot keep them all.

If you know you want a cat but you're not sure where you'll get one, you should consider adopting a cat from an animal shelter or animal rescue. The benefits of adopting a cat as opposed to buying one from a pet store or breeder are numerous. Of course, the greatest thing about adoption is the ability to give a forever home to a cat who may otherwise not have been adopted. Beyond that, many shelter and rescue pets are already socialized, and it costs far less to adopt a cat than to buy from a breeder or pet store.

There are some differences between shelters and rescues to be aware of before making a decision on which to go with:

Animal shelters are physical locations where large numbers of animals are kept while waiting to be rehomed. Pounds run by government organizations are an example of shelters, but there are also privately funded shelters. Animal shelters typically accept any animal that is surrendered, brought in because their owners can no longer take care of them, or found wandering in the streets. Due to the number of animals that shelters accept, many have a policy of only holding an animal for a certain length of time to see if they can be placed before they are euthanized. There are some "no-kill shelters" that do not follow this policy, thankfully.

Adopting a cat from an animal shelter is usually a straightforward process. You can see the sheltered cats when you visit the location, choose one, and then pay a fee to take them home. The fee is to cover the costs of vaccinations and sometimes spaying or neutering. Depending on the shelter, the adoption process may take place the same day you choose a cat.

Animal rescues generally don't operate from a single location. Instead, they are a network of volunteers and foster homes that work together to remove animals from unsafe situations, rehabilitate them, and help them learn to socialize with humans and other pets. They will also treat any medical conditions before clearing the animal for rehoming.

The process of adopting a cat from a rescue is longer than at a shelter and may be more expensive (although it still does not cost as much as buying from a breeder). Animal rescues have procedures to ensure that the cats they rescue are sent to a forever home; often, shelters have problems with people deciding the animals they have adopted aren't "right" and returning them to the shelter. To prevent this from happening, rescues have potential owners spend time with a cat before allowing the adoption. There are background checks, home checks, and usually a trial period where you'll basically foster the cat before officially adopting. Some rescues may also check in periodically after the adoption to ensure things are still going well.

What Should You Know Before Getting a Cat?

There are several things to make sure you have in place before bringing a cat home:

- ✧ Understand what type of cat will do best in your living situation and with the personalities of the humans (and any other pets) who already live there.

- ✧ Know that there is a time commitment involved, and no matter what type of cat you get, you can't just set out food and ignore them. Be prepared to spend some time with your cat to make sure they get enough play and affection.

- ✧ Ensure that your home is a safe environment for your cat, decide ahead of time whether or not the cat will be allowed outside, and take any necessary precautions if you choose to let them out. We will discuss indoor versus outdoor cats in a later chapter.

- ✧ Set up an appointment with a veterinarian who will provide healthcare for your cat.

- ✧ Do not plan to have your cat declawed. If your cat is intact, decide whether or not you will have them spayed or neutered. This is a good conversation to have with your vet.

- ✧ Above all, remember that cats are a lifetime commitment. Indoor cats can live up to 20 years, so you will want to plan accordingly to not give them up for any reason.

Setting Up a Safe Environment for Your Cat

Just like people, your cat will need to feel safe and secure when they arrive in a new home. This means you'll have to make sure you have the things they need before they come home with you in order to make the adjustment period as easy as possible for you and your new cat.

Of course, you will absolutely need to have the basics on hand when your new cat arrives. Ensure you have all the necessary supplies ahead of time, including a food supply, food and water dishes, a litter box and a supply of litter, a scratching post, toys, and treats. You may also want to get a cat bed, but be aware that cats generally sleep wherever they are most comfortable – often, that place is not the cat bed.

You'll also need to ensure enough space for your cat. This doesn't necessarily mean that you have to assign your cat an entire room to themselves (though you certainly can if you want to!), but there should be multiple and separated areas, if possible in low-traffic places of your home, for your cat to eat, use the bathroom, play, and rest. It is highly advisable to give your cat a "safe space", especially when they first arrive, where they can hunker down if they feel anxious. This can be something as simple as a cardboard box with at least two entrances/exits cut into it.

A scratching post is necessary because cats need to sharpen their claws, and if you don't have a designated space for your cat to do this, they will use furniture or walls. At first, you may want to supply multiple scratching surfaces, at least until your cat shows a preference for one over the others. They will often tend to choose one place to scratch.

Finally, when you first bring your cat home, they may need a few days up to a few weeks to adjust to their new surroundings, depending on the individual cat's personality and temperament. If your new cat goes into hiding, don't push them to come out. Instead, be sure that there is food, water, and a litter box available, and keep track to make sure the food is being eaten and the litter box is being used. If these things happen, but you don't actually see your new cat, give them time. They will come out when they're ready.

How to Feed Your Cat

When it comes to feeding your cat, there are two main decisions: what you'll feed them and how often.

What to feed your cat depends on many things. First, if possible, try to find out what kind of food they've been eating prior to joining your family and feed them the same brand/flavor. Consistency is comforting for cats, so the more familiar things you can provide for them, the sooner they'll be able to relax. They may also struggle with digestive issues if you suddenly switch the type of food you feed them. You can transition to another brand by mixing the two types at first, then gradually phasing out the original food brand in favor of the new.

There is also the question of whether to feed your cat dry food, wet food, or both. Both types have advantages and disadvantages. For instance, dry food is good for your cat's dental health and is easier to store, while wet food can help your cat get the moisture they need if they do not drink enough water or if they have a medical condition that requires a higher water intake, such as kidney or urinary issues. Of course, you will also want to consider what your cat enjoys eating!

Finally, you can consider a raw food diet for your cat. We will discuss this in a later chapter.

How often to feed your cat is also dependent on your cat and their eating habits. You'll want to feed them enough so they don't go hungry, but you'll want to avoid obesity, placing your cat at a higher risk for health problems. There are three common approaches to how often you should feed your cat:

Meal feeding: As the name suggests, this is when you provide your cat with food only at specific mealtimes. The advantage to this approach is that you will be able to monitor how much your cat eats to make sure it's enough but not too much. You may use this approach if your cat is prone to packing on extra pounds, but be sure to discuss it with your vet so you know that your cat is getting the right amount of nutrition and not starving. Meal feeding for cats usually involves one to two meals a day, depending on your cat's eating habits and nutritional needs.

Free feeding: In this approach, you simply make your cat's food available at all times, and they can eat when they choose to. Free feeding is only for dry food, as wet food will go bad if left out all day. The best approach to free-feeding is to still provide as much food as your cat will eat in a day, and if there is any left over, discard what's left and fill the bowl with fresh food. Like human food left out of the packaging, dry cat food can become stale when it's exposed.

Combination/mixed feeding: This is a combination of both approaches, where you would leave dry food freely available all day and feed wet food once or twice per day. With this feeding style, cats can enjoy the benefits of both food types. You will just need to monitor your cat and make sure they don't gain excessive weight, leading to health problems.

How to Find a Vet (and Make Your First Vet Visit)

Among the biggest decisions you will make for your new cat is choosing the right veterinarian. Your vet will be important in helping you ensure that your cat enjoys a long and healthy life. Look up local veterinarian offices and find those that have the best locations and hours for you. For example, if you work 9 to 5, you may want a vet who's open later or on weekends.

You should find a vet prior to bringing your cat home. The best first time to visit the vet's office is actually *before* you have your cat. This way, you can get a sense of the office and the people who work there in person, ask questions about their services, and find out if you like them. You don't want to be stuck with a vet whose personality clashes with yours.

In addition, you should plan on bringing your new kitty to the vet soon after you bring them home for a check-up and to discuss a long-term care plan for your cat.

How else can you find a vet? One of the best ways is through word of mouth; ask family and friends who have cats if they can recommend someone for you. You might also look at online reviews, search the American Animal Hospital Association to find any accredited veterinarians near you, or consult your state's veterinary medical association.

Questions to ask potential vets:

- ✧ Do you accept pet insurance (if you plan to get this)?
- ✧ What kind of payment policies do you have?
- ✧ How much does a standard office visit cost?

- Do you accept walk-in care requests?
- Do you handle emergencies or refer them somewhere specific?
- Are you able to perform tests, procedures, and fill prescriptions at your office?
- What about dental care?
- How many veterinarians work at your practice?

Preventative Healthcare for Your Cat

Taking preventative healthcare measures helps your cat stay healthy and happy, and it can extend their life span significantly. In short, preventative healthcare is an approach that assumes it's always better to avoid your cat getting sick in the first place than to treat them after they're sick.

You should discuss your cat's preventative healthcare plan with your vet. In general, it's worth noting that since cats have shorter life spans and age faster than humans, they should see the doctor more often for general check-ins. Young to adult cats should be examined, even when they're healthy, at least once or twice a year. For mature and senior cats, wellness checks should occur more often.

Preventive healthcare measures include health examinations, immunizations, testing for various illnesses and parasites, weight maintenance, and dental care. Also, if you notice changes in your cat's behavior patterns, it's good to check in with your vet and determine whether this is an indicator of a health issue.

Another type of preventative healthcare is avoiding health risks, including parasites and poisons. Parasite prevention involves medication to keep them from getting heartworms or intestinal parasites and an effective method for flea and tick control. Keep in mind that cats allowed outdoors have a greater risk of parasitic infections.

You should also make sure that your cat does not have access to poisonous or toxic substances. Things that are toxic for cats to ingest include:

- **Lilies:** True lilies and daylilies, including Easter, Asiatic, Japanese, and Tiger lilies, are incredibly toxic to cats and may be fatal if swallowed, potentially leading to irreversible kidney failure. "False" lilies such as Calla and Peace lilies are also toxic and cause moderate to severe irritation but are not usually fatal.

- ***Allium* plant species:** Garlic, chives, onions, leeks, scallions, and shallots are toxic to cats.

- **Chocolate:** Fats and sugars, including chocolate, can cause vomiting and diarrhea in cats. Furthermore, a stimulant compound called theobromine found in chocolate can lead to trembling, hyperactivity, and seizures.

- **NSAIDs:** Although NSAIDs (non-steroidal anti-inflammatory drugs) are commonly used to treat dogs and people, this type of drug is among the most deadly for cats. Common NSAIDs include ibuprofen and naproxen. While not an NSAID, Acetaminophen is also toxic and potentially fatal to cats.

- **Vitamin D3:** Both vitamin D supplements and rodent bait containing cholecalciferol can cause poisoning in cats, leading to organ damage and kidney failure.

✧ **Household cleaners:** Many common household cleaners can be toxic to cats. This is not to say you can't use them, but keep products out of your cat's reach and clean up any residue after use. Keep cats away from areas where cleaners have been used until the products are completely dry.

How Do You Know When It's Time to Go to the Vet?

Cats may sometimes cough up hairballs, vomit for no apparent reason, or get into bouts of sneezing without cause for alarm. How do you discern when your cat will be okay and when to head to the vet's office? Here are common symptoms that you shouldn't ignore:

✧ *Repeated vomiting.* It's normal for your cat to occasionally throw up food or hair. However, repeated vomiting (many times over the course of a day) is not normal. If your cat is repeatedly vomiting but still eating, drinking, and using the litter box, you can simply call, but if they are doing none of these things, it's a medical emergency.

✧ *Sudden appetite changes.* It's important to know how much and how often your cat usually eats. If they are suddenly eating a lot more or a lot less than usual, contact your vet to discuss it.

✧ *Runny nose and/or eyes.* If you notice discharge from your cat's nose or eyes, you should get them checked out. Runny eyes/nose combined with sneezing, panting, or shortness of breath is usually a sign of a respiratory infection. Changes to your cat's breathing without discharge also indicates a potential problem that requires vet attention.

✧ *Extreme fatigue.* While cats normally sleep a lot, if you notice your cat seems entirely lethargic or sedentary with no interest in things they normally enjoy, you should make an appointment with your vet.

- ✧ **Litter box behavior changes.** This is a potential problem, especially in male cats, although female cats can develop problems too. You should contact your vet right away if your cat strains to produce little urine, urinates outside a clean litter box, or excessively grooms their genitals.

- ✧ **Obvious signs of distress.** You should talk to your vet if your cat suddenly seems upset and engages in behavior such as crying, howling, hiding, or anything out of character for them.

- ✧ **Lump or growth.** If you notice new lumps or bumps on your cat, these should be checked out by your vet, as they could indicate a tumor.

- ✧ **Back legs dragging.** If your cat is dragging themselves around by their front legs, you need to get to a vet immediately. This is almost always a symptom of aortic thromboembolism, a complication of heart disease that causes distress and paralysis.

- ✧ **Following any major trauma.** If your cat gets into a fight with another animal, is hit by a car, or otherwise experiences trauma, you need to head to the vet's office, even if your cat seems fine afterward. There may be hidden wounds or internal injuries that can lead to infection or worse.

Playtime Tips for Your Cat

All cats need some sort of exercise and mental stimulation to stay healthy and happy. For this reason, playtime is very important. It even makes a great excuse—if you're asked to do something you don't want to, you can say that you have to play with your cat!

To make playtime fun, ensure that you have a good variety of toys on hand and switch out the toys between playtimes, so your cat doesn't end up playing with the same toy repeatedly. A good length for play sessions with your cat is around 10 to 15 minutes each day, two to three times a day.

When finished, it's a good idea to put the toys away until the next play session. If your cat can play with their toys any time, with or without you, they may quickly become bored and no longer interested in them.

Some playtime ideas for your cat:

- Since cats are instinctual hunters, most will enjoy playing "prey" with a teaser wand, jingle ball, or other small toy. Make the toy move with changes in speed, pauses, and slight jerks to mimic wounded prey, and your cat will likely not be able to resist pouncing.

- Ordinary objects like bits of string or yarn can also be fun for cats to play with. Just make sure you don't use an item small enough for your cat to swallow.

- You can use food puzzles to help challenge your cat while also giving them treats. These are great toys for cats who may struggle with their weight.

- ✧ Vertical space is a must for cats, as they enjoy being up high. Consider installing cat shelves or investing in a cat condo to give them space to climb and play.

- ✧ For indoor cats, a bit of supervised outdoor time can also be fun. You may consider a protected, screened-in space in your yard to give your cat some fresh air and sunshine (with accessible toys included) or leash-training them so you can go for short walks together.

Your Cat's Needs: Different Approaches for Different Ages

You will need to vary your approach to caring for your cat at different ages in their lives. Here are some tips on ensuring your kitty's continued health and happiness throughout their life stages.

How to get kittens off to the right start

Kittenhood is a time of change for all cats; this is when they experience more physical and mental changes than any other stage in their lives. When caring for kittens, ensure they have high-quality food meant for kittens to ensure proper nutrition. Assure that they are litter box trained as well since this is when they form toilet habits. It's also important to make sure your kitten is well socialized, with plenty of exposure to new people and experiences, to avoid stress later in life.

Tips for keeping your junior/adult cat happy

Young adult cats are prone to wandering, so at this stage in their lives, it is appropriate to consider whether you will be spaying or neutering your cat. You will also need to replace the litter box with a more age- and size-appropriate model, as your cat will be larger and need more room.

From around 3 to 6 years old, cats are in their prime and don't need as much direct care and supervision. However, they still need enrichment through fun and exercise and continued socialization. They may also require more frequent checkups at the vet, paying additional attention to weight and dental hygiene.

Caring for your senior cat

Mature cats from 7 years and up are less active and will need more frequent health checkups. A number of common physical ailments can start to develop as your cat becomes older, such as problems with hearing and vision or arthritis, and your vet can help you ensure that you keep them healthy. They may not be as active, but older cats still need attention and gentle enrichment.

With senior pets beyond 11 years old, you may find that your cat needs more help getting around and potentially a new litter box style if the height of the current one causes them accessibility issues. Geriatric cats over 15 years old almost inevitably develop some medical issues and should be seen by the vet 2 to 3 times per year.

Tips for Multi-Cat Households

If having one cat is wonderful, having more than one cat must be heaven… unless your kitties decide they don't like each other. Luckily, you can improve relations in your multi-cat household so that everyone gets along. Your multiple cats may never fall in love with each other, but you can certainly stop them from actively trying to get rid of the competition and help them tolerate the presence of other cats.

Although cats have a reputation for being aloof and solitary individuals, they are actually highly social and enjoy the company of other cats. However, cats who don't abide with humans form social groups (colonies) of their own volition; they get to choose who's in the group and who's out. If a feral or stray cat doesn't fit in with a colony, they will move on and look for another colony.

With domestic cats, the choice of who to hang out with is removed because the human decides on the colony population (the "colony," meaning every living being in the household). This means your kitties will depend on you to blend other cats they may view as misfits into a functional family.

Adding multiple cats who are littermates or bonded pairs can help if you plan to adopting more than one cat. But if you already have cats and want to add more, there are ways to help ensure that everyone gets along:

- ✧ Introduce a new cat to your home by keeping them in a room that's separate from other cats for the first few days until both the new cat and the resident cats have gotten used to the changed situation. Allow resident cats to sniff around the door but keep them out of the room at first.

- ✧ Use scent swapping to help your cats get used to one another's scents. With a glove, facecloth, or natural bristle brush, rub your resident cat's chin and cheeks while petting and then use the same item to pet the new cat's cheeks and chin. Then, reverse the process.

- Make sure your cats have plenty of room to move around the house and claim separate territory to escape the other cats as needed. This should include vertical spaces like shelves, bookcases, cat trees and condos, the top of the fridge, or any other place you're comfortable allowing your cats.

- Ensure multiple travel paths throughout your home with different ways to enter and exit each room. This can help curb bully behavior and allow a cat who's being bullied to escape.

- Offer enough enrichment toys so each cat can play individually. Consider providing cat furniture such as tunnels and catios to allow various cats to stake their claims.

- Provide individual attention for each of your cats and group playtime where you encourage the cats to play together.

- If you have a kitten and an older cat, give the baby plenty of playtime so they are worn out enough not to pester your older cat (who often will not want to play with the baby).

- Consider playing calming music that is specifically designed for cats and using diffusers to emulate natural cat pheromones, which helps to reduce stress behaviors like fighting, scratching, hiding, and spraying urine.

- Place multiple resources in different areas of the house – a minimum of one for each cat – including scratching posts and food and water stations. For litter boxes, you'll need at least as many as you have cats, plus one.

- ✧ Be patient and understand that it may take time for your cats to learn to tolerate each other. With encouragement from you, your multiple cats will begin to get along and co-exist peacefully.

Taking great care of your new cat means being aware of the best care routines, as well as the steps to take if your cat encounters problems at any stage of their lives.

In the next chapter, we'll talk about indoor versus outdoor cats and deciding whether you will allow your cat outside.

CHAPTER 8

INDOOR VS. OUTDOOR: WHAT'S PERFECT FOR YOUR CAT?

"I've always wanted to be a cat. Warm and domesticated when you want to be, wild when you don't."

– Jenny Downham

Should you let your cat go outside or keep them indoors at all times? This is a long-standing debate among cat owners. In this chapter, we'll look at the advantages and disadvantages of each choice, as well as a third option you may consider if you want both for your cat.

Factors to Consider in Deciding Whether to Let Your Cat Outside

There are several things you should think about before choosing whether or not your cat will be going outside. These include:

✧ The general safety of the area where you live

- Pet laws that govern your region and may affect your decision
- Whether you live in the city or the country
- The climate of your area (i.e., if it gets too cold, you would not want your cat outside)
- Cultural differences in your area
- The country you live in. For example, a recent international study showed more indoor cats in the U.S. than in much of Europe, with 63% of U.S. cats kept entirely indoors compared to around 26.1% in the U.K. (Foreman-Worsley, 2021).

One other factor to consider is the personality of your cat. Some cats prefer the ability to go outside, while others may become anxious in unfamiliar environments and would rather stay indoors.

The Pros and Cons of Keeping Your Cat Indoors vs. Letting Your Cat Outside

Among the advantages of keeping your cat indoors is minimized risk exposure. Cats allowed to roam freely outdoors have increased chances of being infected with parasites, ingesting toxic or poisonous substances, being attacked by other animals, and being struck by traffic. Indoor cats have a greatly reduced risk of contracting diseases spread by other cats, such as feline immunodeficiency virus (FIV) and feline leukemia virus (FeLV or FLV). Also, outdoor cats may become lost and suffer from exposure to the elements. There is also a greater risk of your cat getting trapped in an outbuilding or another house or falling asleep somewhere that poses a hazard (such as on top of car tires or inside engine bays) – as cats enjoy sleeping in warm, confined spaces.

Other people can also pose a hazard to a freely roaming outdoor cat. If your cat is friendly and goes outside, someone else may decide to "adopt" them. People may also turn in cats who appear to be strays to an animal shelter, and you will typically have to pay a fee to get them back – if you find out they've been surrendered to a shelter at all.

Another issue with outdoor cats is the danger they impose. Cats are notorious hunters, and killing animals such as birds poses a threat to the local wildlife and ecosystem.

However, there are some potential disadvantages to keeping your cat indoors. Scientists believe that cats are only semi-domesticated, which can mean they may become frustrated by being "cooped up" inside all the time. They might experience behavioral issues such as excessive scratching or spraying. Indoor cats also have a higher risk for obesity. Finally, if an indoor cat does "escape" outside, they may become lost due to being unfamiliar with the territory.

Allowing your cat to spend time outside can have a few benefits. The ability to be outside may curb some instinctive behaviors such as scratching and hunting. They will often engage in more physical activity, which helps to reduce the risk of obesity. Additionally, going outside allows cats to sharpen their claws unreservedly and scent mark a wider territory.

How to Decrease Risks for Outdoor Cats

There are some ways you can help to decrease the risks associated with letting your cat outside. Having your cat microchipped is important (for indoor cats as well!) because if they become lost or injured and another person brings them to a shelter or veterinarian, they will be able to identify you as the owner and contact you. You may additionally want to have your cat wear a collar with ID tags listing your name and contact information for the same purpose.

Preventative healthcare is especially important for cats who go outdoors. You'll want to protect them as much as possible from diseases and parasites. Although there are no preventative measures for some types of cat illness, you should provide as many options for preventing parasites and disease.

Consider having your cat spayed or neutered if you plan to let them outside. This will prevent unwanted pregnancy, reduce the risk of sexually transmitted diseases (yes, cats can get them!), and curb spraying behavior in males. Having your cat fixed may also limit their wandering radius so they'll stick closer to home while they're outside, as they will not be looking for a mate.

You should also let your neighbors know you have an outdoor cat to ensure they know who your cat belongs to and whether they would have an issue with your cat entering their property. You might try to see if any neighbors have pets who could harm your cat, such as dogs who may be unsocialized to cats.

If you intend to allow your cat outside when you are not home, you should consider installing a cat flap so your cat can return during inclement weather or if they feel threatened, even when you aren't there to let them in.

Furthermore, consider leash training your cat so that their outside time is more supervised and comes with lower risks.

Best of Both Worlds: Building a Cattery

If you don't want your cat exposed to the risks of being outside but still want them to experience the outdoors and gain some of the benefits, you might consider building a cattery, which is an outdoor enclosure designed for cats. There are many different types of catteries, from simple wood frames enclosed with mesh (the cat-proof variety, of course!) to elaborate outdoor cat condos equipped with perches and stimulation equipment. Your cat will be able to enjoy the outdoors safely while burning off excess energy that may build up from being indoors for long periods of time.

Unfortunately, the ability to use this option depends on your yard space and how much money you are able to spend. Catteries can be expensive, but some types don't have to be. You can build a cattery yourself with lumber and mesh screening. If you don't have the space for such a project, you might consider building a small "cat porch" connected to your house – a screened structure similar to a cattery, with more vertical space than horizontal, where your cat can at least get some fresh air and climbing exercise.

In the next chapter, we'll take a look at raw food diets for cats and whether they can be beneficial, if you choose to feed this way.

CHAPTER 9

PET FOOD PROBLEMS: WHY YOU SHOULD CONSIDER A RAW DIET FOR YOUR CAT

"Eat every meal as though it were your last."

– Garfield

Is commercial pet food the right choice for your cat, or should you consider feeding them raw foods? This topic is often debated. One thing to note here is that cats are obligate carnivores – they *must* consume meat to satisfy their nutritional needs. Commercial pet food provides the nutrients your cat needs, but it also contains fillers and other unnecessary components, and the protein contained in wet and dry cat food is not always of the highest quality.

Pet Health Problems and the Pet Food Industry

There are two main issues with commercial pet food brands: the quality of the protein source used for the pet food and the amount of fillers added to the formula.

You can see the issues with protein sources in cat food brands when trying to decipher the ingredients list on the label. Ideally, pet food that is low in fillers and high in quality protein would list the ingredients (arranged from highest to lowest content in the formula) like the main protein source, secondary protein source, then fillers, fats, preservatives, vitamins and minerals, and taurine to indicate lower contents of these ingredients.

However, some cat foods list fillers directly after the main protein source – or worse, list "meat products" as the first ingredient and, therefore primary protein source. "Meat products" refers to any animal parts left over after processing quality meat. This means many brands of cat food consist primarily of poor quality protein and fillers, which may include corn, soy, rice, and grain ingredients. These often increase the overall protein count in the pet food; however, cats do not naturally consume these foods, and plant-based ingredients can have a negative impact on your cat's health – not to mention the sugar, salt, and fats that are added to commercial pet food.

Some of the common cat illnesses linked to commercial cat food diets include:

Obesity: While fat cats are adorable, they are unfortunately not healthy. Obesity in cats can lead to a wide variety of health problems and shorten your pet's lifespan significantly. The fats and sugars contained in some commercial pet food brands heighten the risk of obesity.

Diarrhea: It's not unusual for cats to suffer the occasional bout of diarrhea. However, there are two main types of diarrhea – small bowel and large bowel. Small bowel diarrhea results in large amounts of loose stool, while large bowel diarrhea forces the cat to strain and produce only small amounts, leading to harmful digestive issues. The latter type is often caused by high-fat content and insoluble (hard to digest) ingredients used in commercial cat food.

Feline lower urinary tract disease (FLUTD): FLUTD is a collection of diseases that cause similar symptoms, such as decreased appetite, general irritation, repeated attempts to urinate without producing anything, and urinating outside the litter box, difficult or painful urination, or bloody urine. Irritation to the urinary tract can be brought on by stress but is also caused or exacerbated by excess body weight and poor diet. It is especially common in cats who are fed only dry food, as the moisture in wet food helps to keep cats hydrated.

Pancreatitis: This inflammation of the pancreas in cats causes digestive enzymes to travel outside the pancreas and break down proteins and necessary fats in other organs, which leads to malnourishment and other health issues. Pancreatitis can be caused by high-fat content and insoluble ingredients in a cat's diet.

Heart disease: Too much salt in your cat's diet can lead to heart disease, just as it can in humans. An increase in water retention caused by high sodium intake leads to elevated blood pressure and an overworked heart, which can significantly shorten your cat's life span.

A Holistic Approach: The Raw Food (Carnivore) Diet

The raw food diet, also called the carnivore diet, involves feeding your cat all the protein and nutrients they need to stay healthy without the fillers and fats that can lead to illness and lowered quality of life.

It's important to note here what a raw food diet is *not*, which is simply feeding raw meat to your cat. A nutritionally balanced raw food diet does require certain nutrients, such as taurine, that are not typically found in meat meant for humans. Additionally, there is a harmful myth that animals can't get food poisoning – they can, and they do. Giving your cat meat that is too spoiled for human consumption will make them sick, at a minimum, and may cause permanent long-term damage.

In order to offer your cat a well-balanced raw food diet, you must include the following components:

- ✧ High-quality proteins and fats
- ✧ Small amounts of vegetables to provide both antioxidants and soluble fiber (nutrients that cats who hunt whole prey consume as a byproduct)
- ✧ Natural trace vitamins, minerals, and fatty acids
- ✧ Taurine (a critical amino acid cats use for digestion, vision, heart muscle function, and immune system health)
- ✧ A high moisture content

Typical high-quality raw food diets for cats include organ meat, raw muscle meat, and ground bones. The best meat sources are often chicken, fish, and eggs, although some raw food diets may include wildfowl, rabbit, or other protein sources that humans do not usually consume.

In addition to raw meat, a balanced carnivore diet should consist of added taurine, vitamin E, vitamin B, and water for extra moisture content. Many recipes also include the addition of salmon oil as a secondary source of protein that also provides necessary fatty acids for cats.

You can find many raw food recipes online, which can be prepared in large batches and frozen so that you can portion them out over weeks, rather than mixing a new meal every day. Alternatively, there are several services that deliver raw pet food to your home, ready to serve or freeze for later consumption.

We will discuss raw food diets in much greater detail in our upcoming book on the perfect diet for your pets. In the meantime, the next chapter discusses how to prepare for major situations and events with your cat, so you're not blindsided by any curveballs that life may throw at you.

CHAPTER 10

FELINE 911: A SURVIVAL GUIDE FOR CAT OWNERS

> "Cats may walk by themselves, but there are times when they need our support."
>
> – Nicholas Dodman

Owning a cat is both a reward and a responsibility. It's important to be prepared for major situations that can affect your cat, such as life events like vacations and moving, as well as potential medical emergencies. In this chapter, we'll go over steps you can take to ensure you're ready to face big challenges with your cat and come out ahead.

Moving to a New Home

Moving is a stressful time for humans, and it is hard on your cat as well. Most cats are more change-averse than people, and many become anxious with slight changes in their routine or environment. This means a major disruption like uprooting and moving permanently to a new place will be highly unsettling for your kitty. If there's a household move in your near future, here are some things you can do to prepare your cat for the big day and help them get used to your new home with as little stress as possible.

Update your cat's ID: One of the biggest issues owners find with moving cats to a new place is frequent escape attempts. Your cat may make a dash for the exit, hoping to find their way back to the familiar home. If this happens despite precautions, you'll want to make sure you can find them. Having a microchip is best, in which case you'll need to update your information on file. Make sure their ID tag is updated with the new address.

Create a new normal: Cats are sensitive to changes in their environment; there are a lot of those happening when you're moving. One thing you can do to help cut down on the stress for your cat is to bring in boxes in advance of packing and keep them around the house. This helps your cat get used to the idea of physical environment changes.

Acclimate to the carrier: It is notoriously difficult getting a cat into a carrier – unless they're used to it. Have a roomy, comfortable cat carrier for your move, and introduce your cat to the carrier a few weeks prior. Place the carrier open in a quiet area of your home, and furnish it with a comfortable blanket or pad, toys, and treats to encourage your cat to go inside. They'll get used to the idea, and the carrier will hold familiar scents, so they'll be less uncomfortable when it's time to move. If you have a long drive to your new home, you should also bring your cat in the carrier on a few car rides prior to moving.

On moving day: Keep your cat in the carrier while all the moving activity is happening and as out of the way from the action as possible. They should stay in the carrier for the drive to the new place and once you've arrived while moving things into your new home. It's tempting to open the carrier mid-move and soothe your upset cat, but resist the temptation... You don't want them bolting in an unfamiliar area.

Introduce the new home: After you've gotten everything inside your new place and cat-proofed things, make sure all windows and external doors are closed, then introduce your cat to one room first. Choose a room where you've placed familiar furniture and objects, and make sure the designated room has food, water, and a litter box. Spend some time with your cat in this room. If your kitty is especially nervous, you may want to keep them in one room for a few days before letting them explore the rest of the house.

Vacation Care for Your Cat

Arranging pet care when you're going on vacation is another common issue. Some believe it's okay to simply leave cats alone, as long as they have access to enough food and water to last until you get back. However, this is *not* a good idea for several reasons: the food and water supply can get contaminated, the litter box will fill and cause accidents, and your cat will be anxious without their humans around. They may engage in destructive behaviors or try harder than usual to escape the house.

If you plan to leave your cats home, arrange for someone to come to your house at least once per day to scoop the litter box, put out fresh food and water, and ensure your cat gets some attention and playtime. You should also leave a radio or television on at low volume, preferably playing cat-friendly programming, and leave a few lights on in key places such as food areas.

Finally, you should not use this arrangement if you will be gone for more than a few days. Some better alternatives for cat vacation care include:

Getting a pet sitter: You can find a professional pet sitter to stay at your home, visit regularly, or bring your cat into their home. There are several Facebook groups offering networking to find vacation pet care in your area.

Kennel care: Pet kennels are boarding houses for pets who need temporary housing. If you choose to leave your cat at a kennel, research potential kennels thoroughly and get recommendations from people who have used them. Some kennels simply place pets in cages and leave them there until their owners return, only providing the minimum necessities.

Cattery: A cattery is a boarding house-type arrangement specifically for cats, where both indoor and protected outdoor spaces are provided, along with individual attention (and, of course, food and water). They tend to be the more expensive option and the least stressful and most enriching experience for your cat.

Emergency Vet Services and Feline First Aid

Cat medical emergencies can be terrifying. If something becomes seriously wrong with your cat, it's crucial to know ahead of time exactly where you're going to take them. The best option is to choose a vet that provides after-hours care or on-call emergency services, so in an emergency, you can take your cat to their regular doctor.

If you don't have that option, familiarize yourself with the closest pet emergency facilities and their respective quality of care. If you have a medical emergency with your cat, call the facility first and let them know you're coming. Even if they are open 24 hours, a quick phone call gives them time to prepare for your cat's arrival and may even save their lives. With issues such as profuse bleeding or cases where you need to induce vomiting, when every minute counts, the vet can walk you through stabilizing your cat on the phone before you bring them in.

Be sure to keep your cat's medical records somewhere that's easily accessible so you can grab them quickly if you need to visit an emergency vet.

Cat First Aid Tips

Here's what you should know about first aid for cats:

Keep a **pet first aid kit** in your car so you can provide immediate treatment if the vet recommends taking steps before bringing your cat in. You can purchase a complete kit or put one together by picking up individual items in a pet first aid kit.

If an emergency occurs, try to **stay as calm as possible** so you can assess things and remove any additional threats to your cat.

For most emergencies (except heatstroke), you'll want to **keep your cat as warm and quiet as possible** and limit movement as much as you can.

Choose a **container with a large opening** to transport an injured cat, such as a sturdy cardboard box or a cat carrier with a removable top. Do *not* force an injured cat through a small opening or door. Once settled, spread a thick towel or blanket over your cat.

Speak in a calm, soothing voice throughout the process to help ease your cat's stress and anxiety about the situation.

If your cat is **showing signs of shock** (rapid heart rate with weak pulse, rapid and/or noisy breathing, listlessness, vomiting, cool extremities including ears and limbs, or pale mucous membranes in the lips, gums, and under eyelids), use blankets or towels to conserve heat and follow the ABCs of first aid:

- ✧ **Airways:** Clear anything obstructing your cat's airway, such as foreign material or vomit.

- ✧ **Breathing:** If your cat does not seem to be breathing, you can gently pump their chest using the palm of your hand while placing your fingers just behind the elbow to check for their pulse. If you don't detect a pulse, you can give your cat rescue breathing.

- ✧ **Cardiac function:** If your cat's heartbeat is slow, weak, or undetected, elevate the lower half of your cat's body (except if there is a spinal injury) while pressing on the chest with your palm and performing rescue breathing.

For unresponsive cats, you can **perform rescue breathing** to help them:

- ✧ Pull the tongue carefully out of the mouth

- ✧ Gently place the head and neck so they are straight. However, if your cat has suffered clear head or neck trauma, *do not* move the head.

- ✧ Clear the mouth carefully of any obstructions or debris.

- ✧ While holding the mouth shut, place your hand over your cat's muzzle and carefully extend the neck. Alternatively, you can use a Styrofoam cup with a large hole poked in the bottom and place the cup opening over your cat's face, pressing gently down to form a tight seal.

- ✧ Blow into your cat's nostrils, either through your hand or the opening in the cup, for two to three breaths, and watch your cat's chest. If there is no rise in the chest, reposition the neck and try again or search for any airway obstructions.

- ✧ If there appears to be an unseen obstruction, try turning your cat upside down, place their back against your chest, and thrust their ribcage sharply five times to attempt to expel any object that may be blocking the airway.

- ✧ For unresponsive cats with no obstructions, continue rescue breathing through your hand or cup at a rate of 20 breaths per minute.

If you believe your cat has been **poisoned or swallowed toxic substances**, contact your vet or a pet poison helpline immediately for further instructions, depending on the type of toxin your cat has been exposed to.

If your cat is **bleeding severely**, try to stop it by applying absorbent clothing or bandages and go to the emergency vet right away. Bleeding wounds require immediate treatment to prevent infection, complications, and bleeding out.

For all cases of medical or health issues, even if you're not sure it's a major problem, it's best to discuss your cat's issues with your veterinarian as soon as possible. This way, you can help prevent minor medical issues from developing into major illnesses or debilitating conditions, ensuring that your cat remains as healthy as possible.

FiNAL WORDS

"How we behave toward cats here below determines our status in heaven."

– Robert A. Heinlein

There is no doubt that cats are amazing. Our feline friends are highly intelligent, very affectionate, and completely adorable. It's true that cats are more independent than dogs and can take care of themselves, but the incredible thing is they *choose* to let us care for them. And they truly care for us a great deal in return.

Although your cat's plaintive cries over their empty food bowl may suggest differently, cats often prefer human attention to food. A study from Oregon State University found that when cats were denied food, toys, scents, and human interaction and then reintroduced to all four stimuli after a few hours, 50 percent of the cats ignored the toys, scents, and even the food; instead, they went straight for love (Vitale Shreve, 2017).

As cat owners, we have the responsibility and the privilege to provide the best for our feline family members. This book is designed to help you do just that. And while some of the solutions provided here may not work for every cat, you can still use this knowledge to learn more about how your cat communicates with you. Meeting your cat's needs becomes far easier when you learn to understand what they're trying to say. In turn, you can deepen your bond with your cat and discover everything these fantastic pets have to offer.

With a cat (or several cats) in your life, you're always a better person for it.

We hope this book helps you create a happy and harmonious everyday life with your cat – a wonderful experience you can enjoy for a long time to come.

Because at the end of the day, there is nothing in the world like snuggling up with a warm cat.

Thank You
FOR YOUR PURCHASE

Thank you for buying our product. It means a lot that you selected our book. THANK YOU for reading all the way through.

Just a quick request before you go. Would you mind posting a review on the platform? Reviewing an independent author's work is the easiest and most direct way to support their work.

Our goal is to continue writing books to help you achieve the results you desire.

ALSO BY

If you loved our book, you might also enjoy
the other books in the series.

RESOURCES

Driscoll, C. A., Menotti-Raymond, M., Roca, A.L, et al. 2007. "The Near Eastern Origin of Cat Domestication." *Science, 317(5837)*; 519-523.

Foreman-Worsley, R., Finka, L.R., Ward, S.J., & Farnworth, M.J. 2021. "Indoors or Outdoors? An International Exploration of Owner Demographics and Decision Making Associated with Lifestyle of Pet Cats." *Animals (Basel), 11(2)*; 253.

Fox, M. W. 2021. *cat. Encyclopedia Britannica.*

Litchfield, C.A., Quinton, G., Tindle, H., Chiera, B., et al. (2017, August 23). "The 'Feline Five': An exploration of personality in pet cats." (*Felis catus*). *PLoS One.*

PetMD Editorial. 2014. "5 Common Cat Illnesses that are Impacted by Nutrition." *PetMD.*

Qureshi, A.I., Memon, M.Z., Vazquez, G., & Suri, M.F. 2009. "Cat ownership and the Risk of Fatal Cardiovascular Diseases. Results from the Second National Health and Nutrition Examination Study Mortality Follow-up Study." *Journal of Vascular and Interventional Neurology, 2(1)*; 132-135.

Stony Brook University. 2017. "Origin of modern dog has a single geographic origin, study reveals." *ScienceDaily*.

Syufy, F. 2019. "The Ingredients in Cat Food: Unraveling the Mystery of Cat Food Ingredients." *The Spruce Pets*.

The International Cat Association. 2018. "Browse All Breeds." *The International Cat Association*.

Vitale Shreve, K.R., Mehrkam, L.R., & Udell, M.A.R. 2017. "Social interaction, food, scent or toys? A formal assessment of domestic pet and shelter cat (*Felis silvestris catus*) preferences." *Behavioral Processes 141(1)*, 322-328. doi:

Printed in Great Britain
by Amazon